Problems of a New Nation

1800–1830

SADDLEBACK
EDUCATIONAL PUBLISHING

Saddleback's *Graphic American History*

SADDLEBACK
EDUCATIONAL PUBLISHING
www.sdlback.com

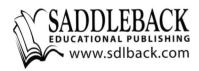

ISBN: 978-1-59905-359-2
eBook: 978-1-60291-687-6

Printed in Malaysia
25 24 23 22 21   10 11 12 13 14

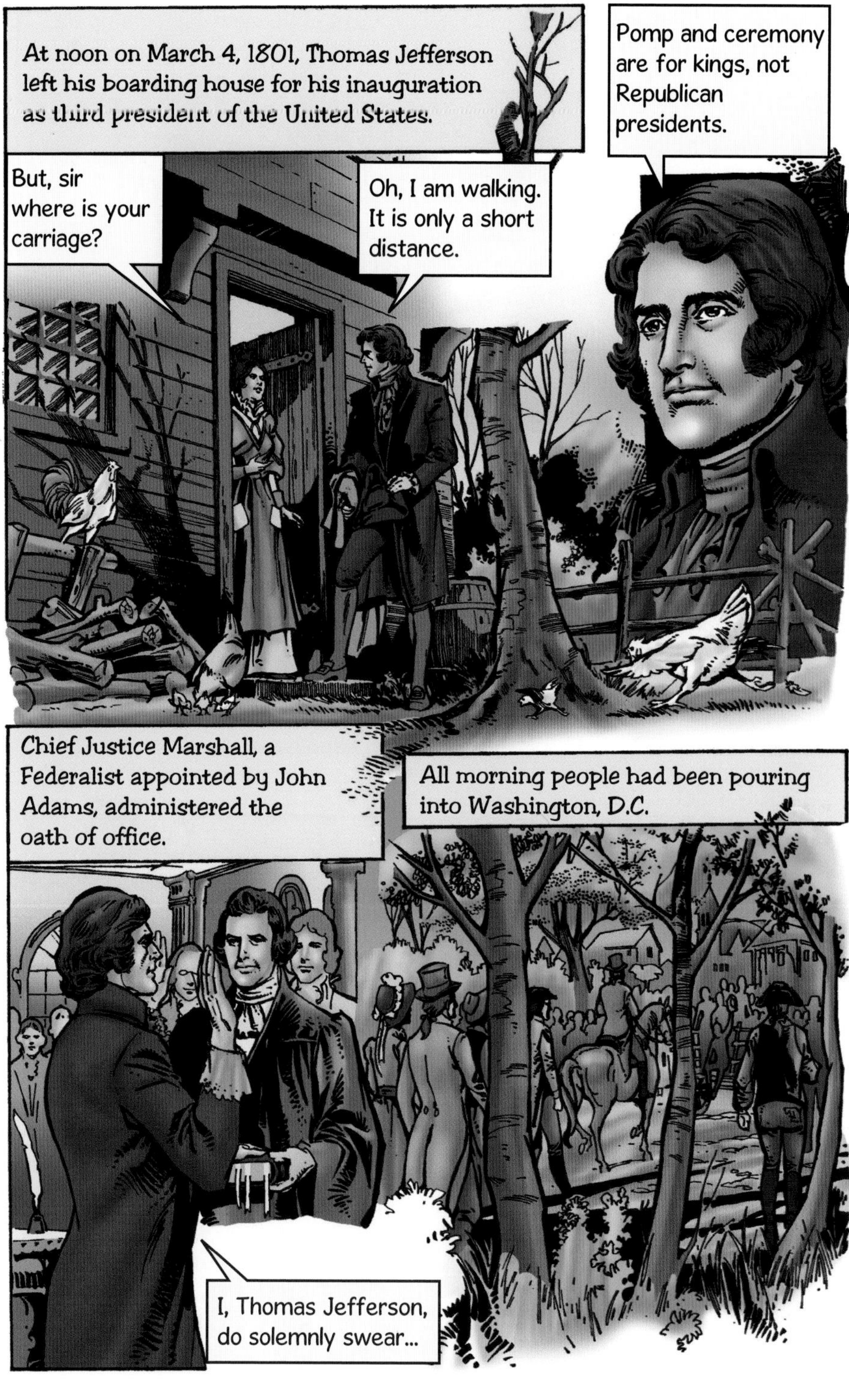

At noon on March 4, 1801, Thomas Jefferson left his boarding house for his inauguration as third president of the United States.
Pomp and ceremony are for kings, not Republican presidents.
But, sir where is your carriage?
Oh, I am walking. It is only a short distance.
Chief Justice Marshall, a Federalist appointed by John Adams, administered the oath of office.
All morning people had been pouring into Washington, D.C.
I, Thomas Jefferson, do solemnly swear...

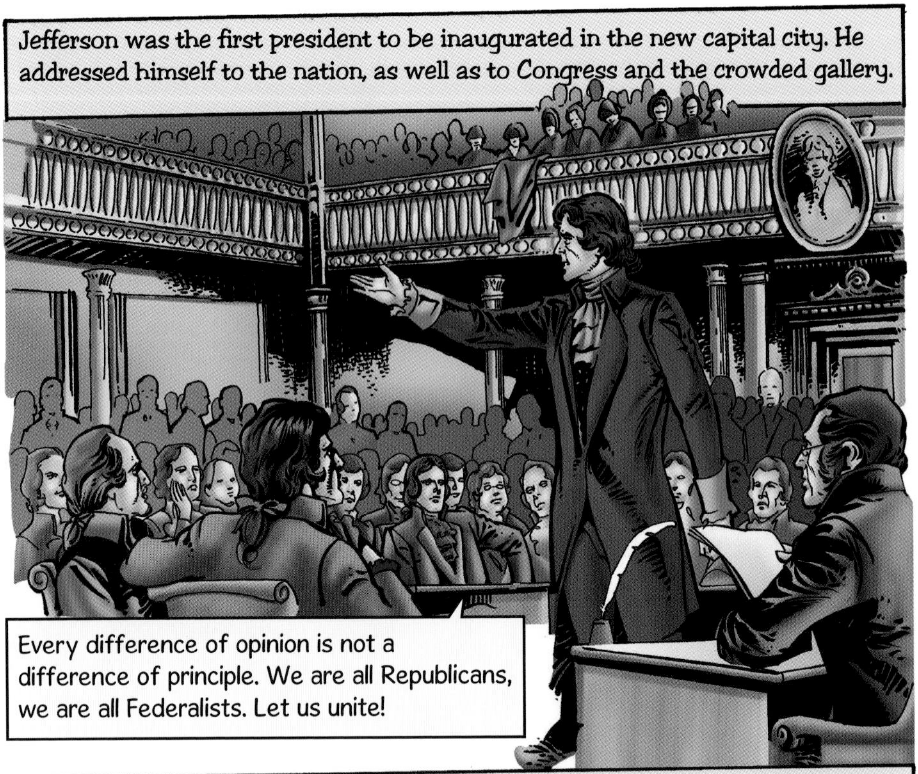
Jefferson was the first president to be inaugurated in the new capital city. He addressed himself to the nation, as well as to Congress and the crowded gallery.
Every difference of opinion is not a difference of principle. We are all Republicans, we are all Federalists. Let us unite!

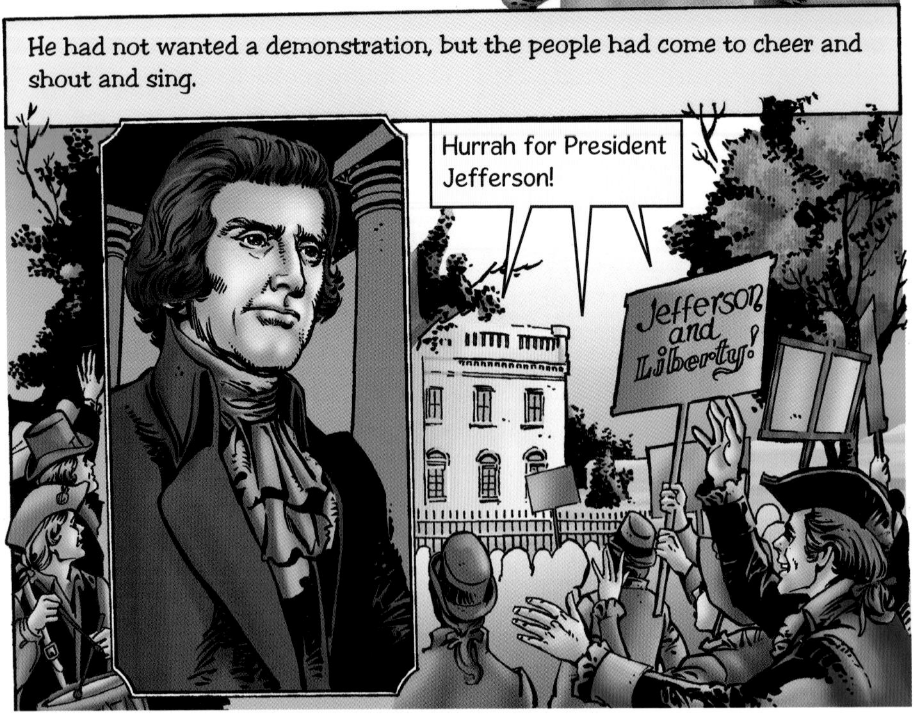
He had not wanted a demonstration, but the people had come to cheer and shout and sing.
Hurrah for President Jefferson!
Jefferson and Liberty!

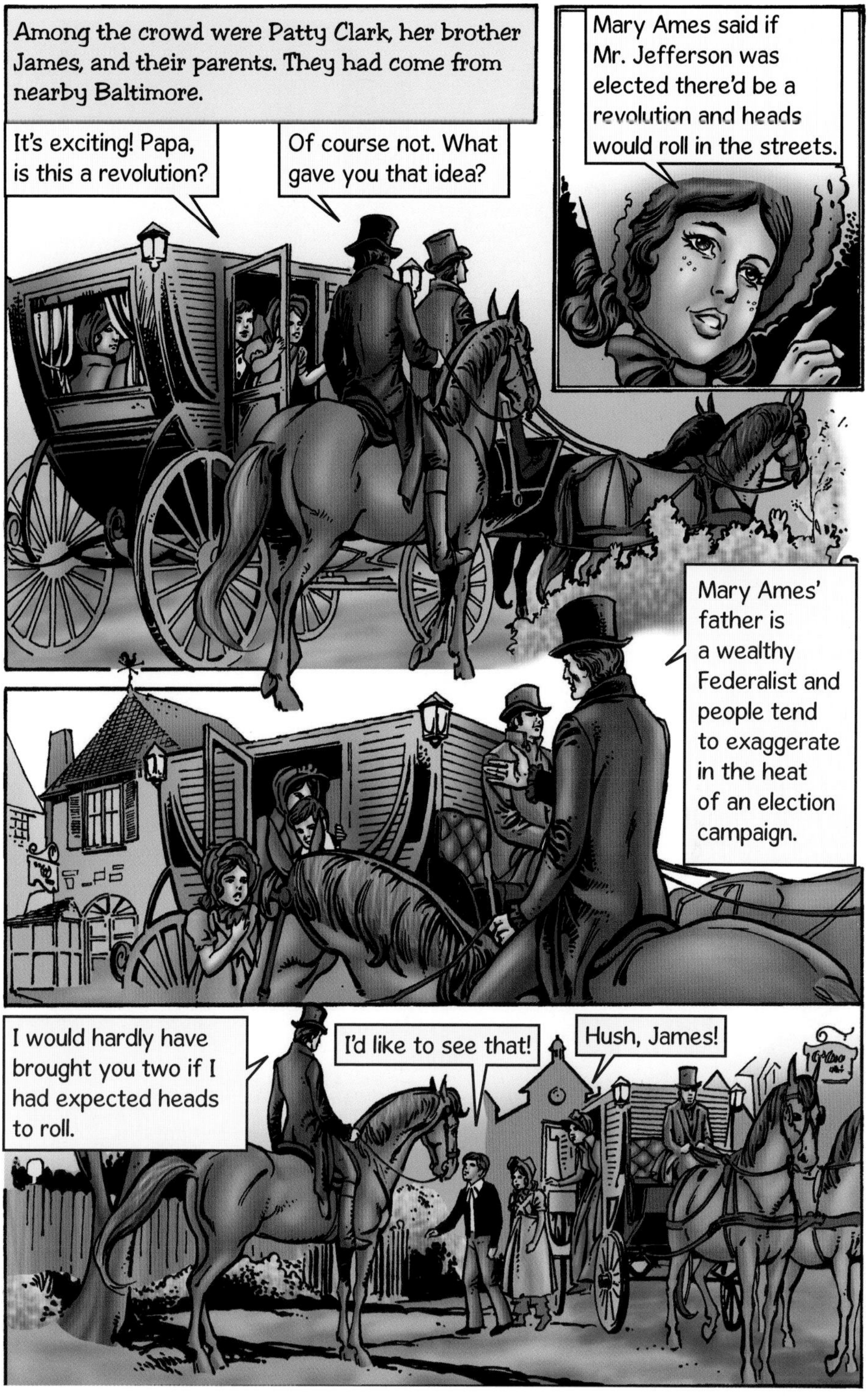
Among the crowd were Patty Clark, her brother James, and their parents. They had come from nearby Baltimore.
It's exciting! Papa, is this a revolution?
Of course not. What gave you that idea?
Mary Ames said if Mr. Jefferson was elected there'd be a revolution and heads would roll in the streets.
Mary Ames' father is a wealthy Federalist and people tend to exaggerate in the heat of an election campaign.
I would hardly have brought you two if I had expected heads to roll.
I'd like to see that!
Hush, James!

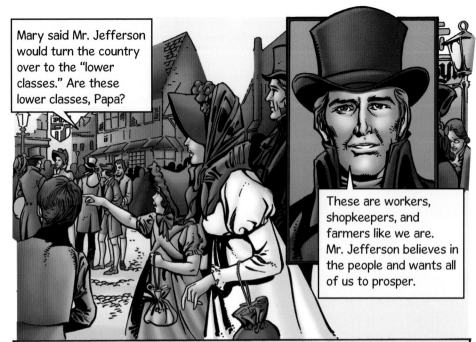

Mary said Mr. Jefferson would turn the country over to the "lower classes." Are these lower classes, Papa?

These are workers, shopkeepers, and farmers like we are. Mr. Jefferson believes in the people and wants all of us to prosper.

Among the first acts of Jefferson's administration were the repeals of the whiskey tax and the Naturalization Act. People imprisoned under the Sedition Act were pardoned.

James Madison was appointed secretary of state.

It is not what the Federalists hoped to get under their sedition law!

And now you are the president!

But the goals set for the new secretary of the treasury, Albert Gallatin, were conservative.

We must reduce government spending, reduce the national debt, lower taxes.

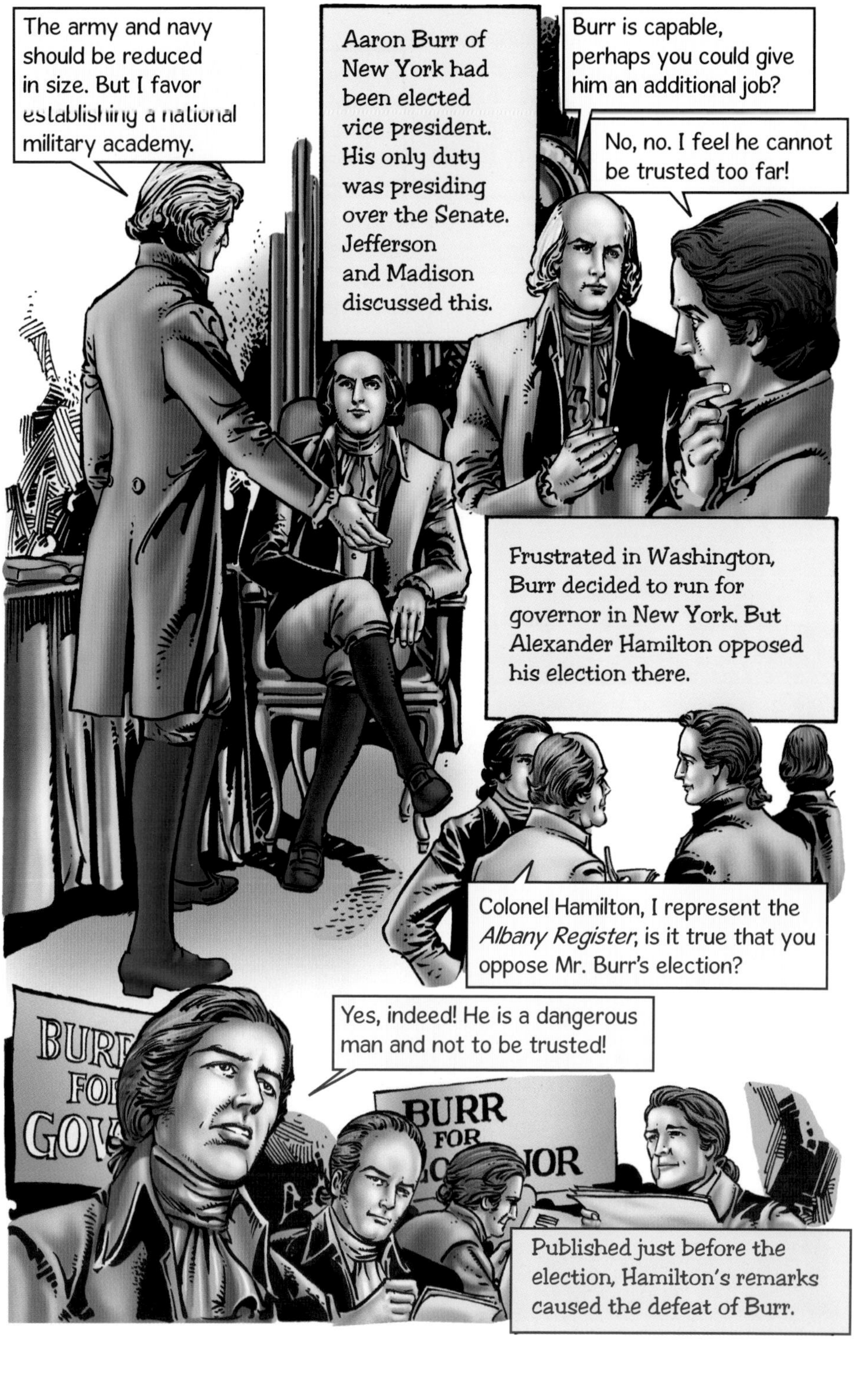
The army and navy should be reduced in size. But I favor establishing a national military academy.
Aaron Burr of New York had been elected vice president. His only duty was presiding over the Senate. Jefferson and Madison discussed this.
Burr is capable, perhaps you could give him an additional job?
No, no. I feel he cannot be trusted too far!
Frustrated in Washington, Burr decided to run for governor in New York. But Alexander Hamilton opposed his election there.
Colonel Hamilton, I represent the *Albany Register*, is it true that you oppose Mr. Burr's election?
Yes, indeed! He is a dangerous man and not to be trusted!
BURR FOR
Published just before the election, Hamilton's remarks caused the defeat of Burr.

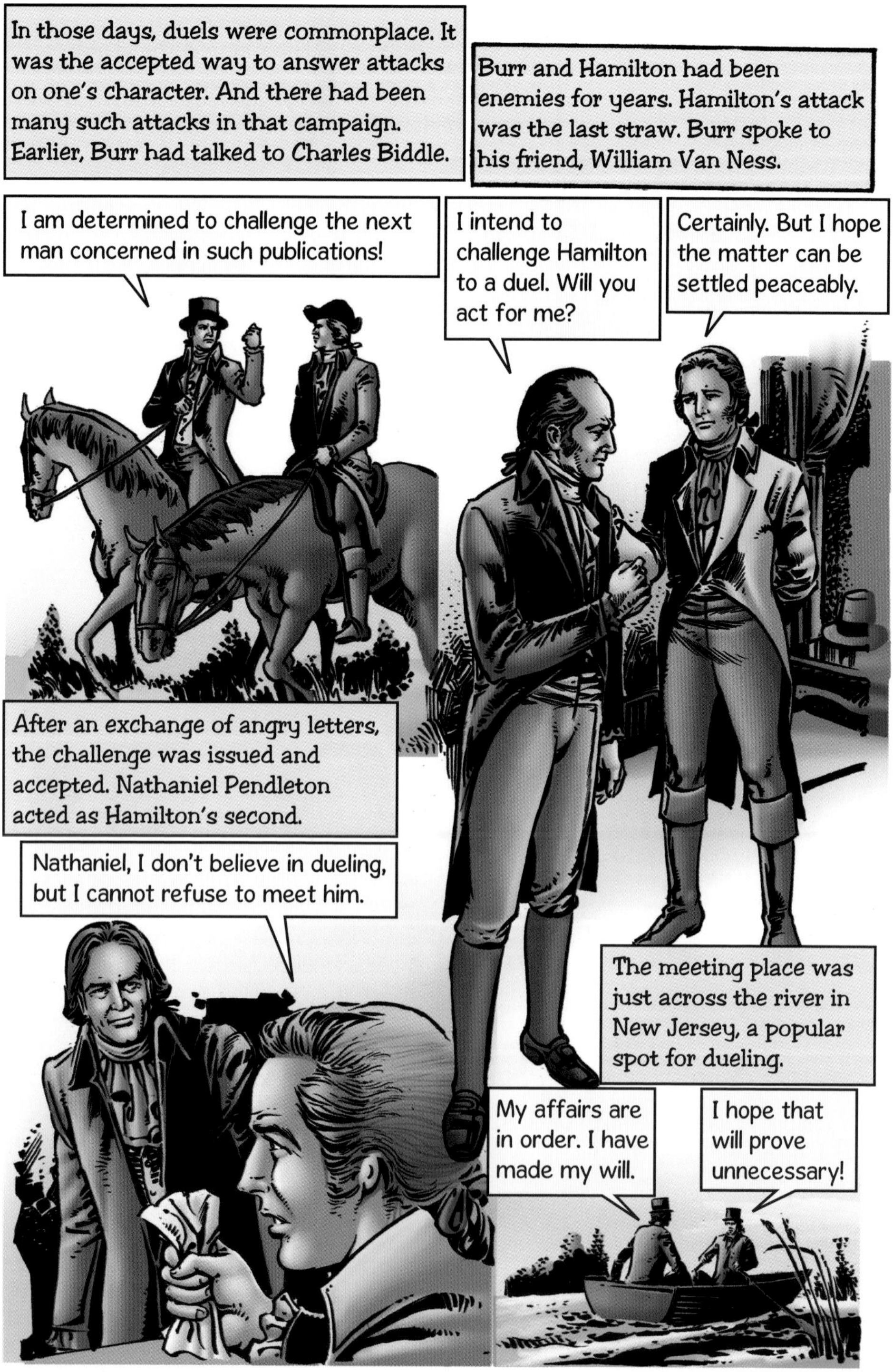
In those days, duels were commonplace. It was the accepted way to answer attacks on one's character. And there had been many such attacks in that campaign. Earlier, Burr had talked to Charles Biddle.
I am determined to challenge the next man concerned in such publications!
Burr and Hamilton had been enemies for years. Hamilton's attack was the last straw. Burr spoke to his friend, William Van Ness.
I intend to challenge Hamilton to a duel. Will you act for me?
Certainly. But I hope the matter can be settled peaceably.
After an exchange of angry letters, the challenge was issued and accepted. Nathaniel Pendleton acted as Hamilton's second.
Nathaniel, I don't believe in dueling, but I cannot refuse to meet him.
The meeting place was just across the river in New Jersey, a popular spot for dueling.
My affairs are in order. I have made my will.
I hope that will prove unnecessary!

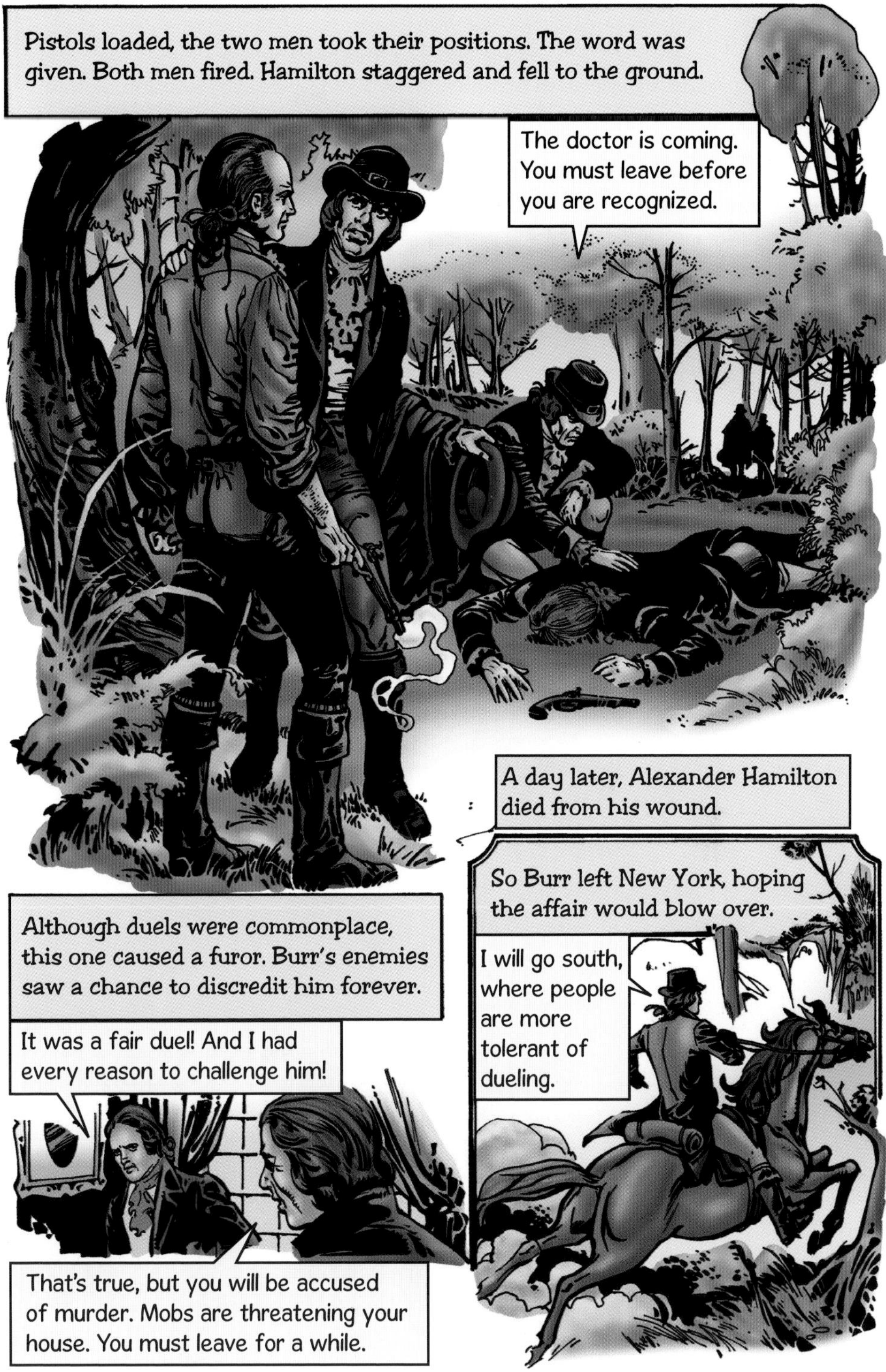
Pistols loaded, the two men took their positions. The word was given. Both men fired. Hamilton staggered and fell to the ground.
The doctor is coming. You must leave before you are recognized.
A day later, Alexander Hamilton died from his wound.
Although duels were commonplace, this one caused a furor. Burr's enemies saw a chance to discredit him forever.
It was a fair duel! And I had every reason to challenge him!
That's true, but you will be accused of murder. Mobs are threatening your house. You must leave for a while.
So Burr left New York, hoping the affair would blow over.
I will go south, where people are more tolerant of dueling.

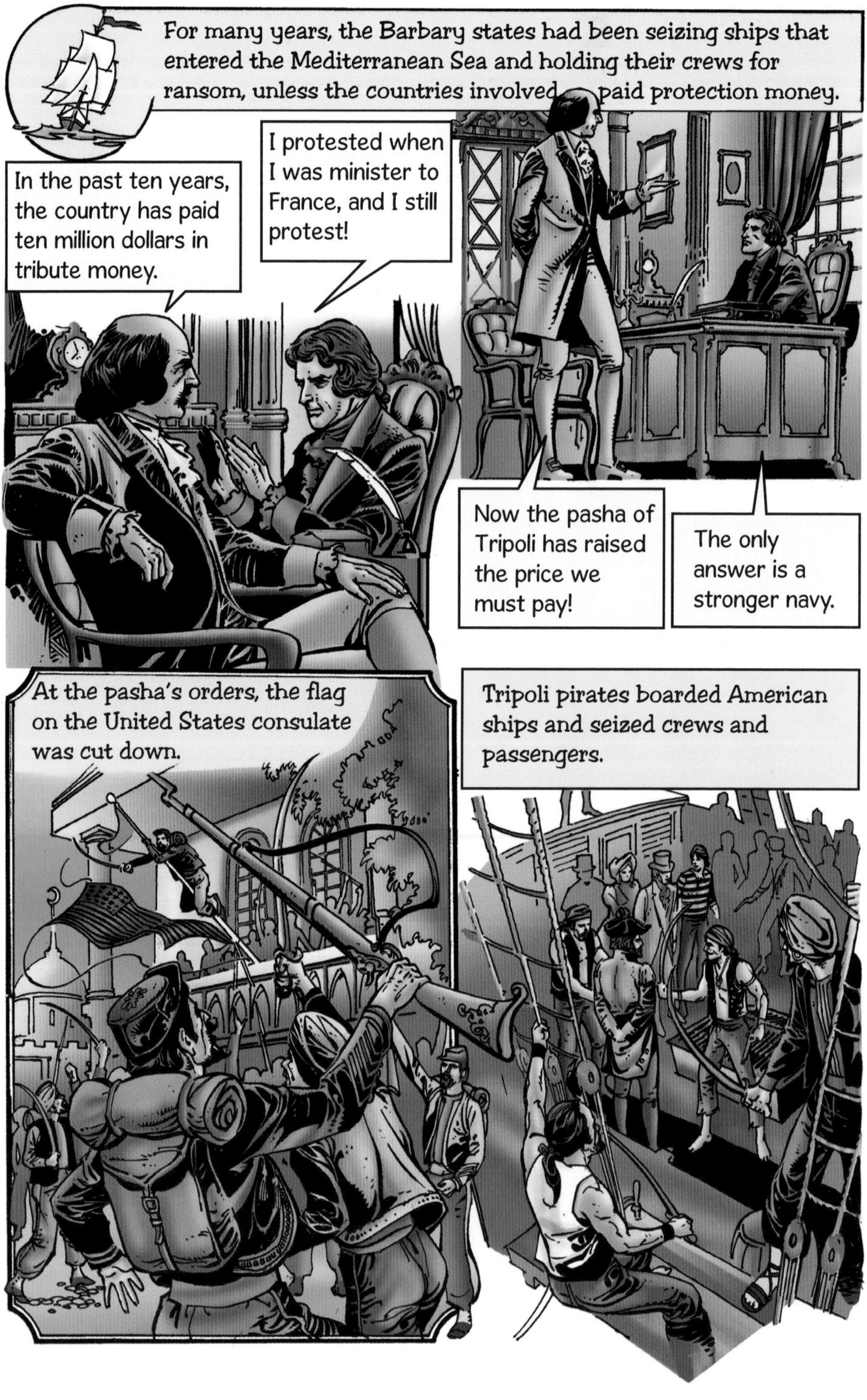
For many years, the Barbary states had been seizing ships that entered the Mediterranean Sea and holding their crews for ransom, unless the countries involved paid protection money.
In the past ten years, the country has paid ten million dollars in tribute money.
I protested when I was minister to France, and I still protest!
Now the pasha of Tripoli has raised the price we must pay!
The only answer is a stronger navy.
At the pasha's orders, the flag on the United States consulate was cut down.
Tripoli pirates boarded American ships and seized crews and passengers.

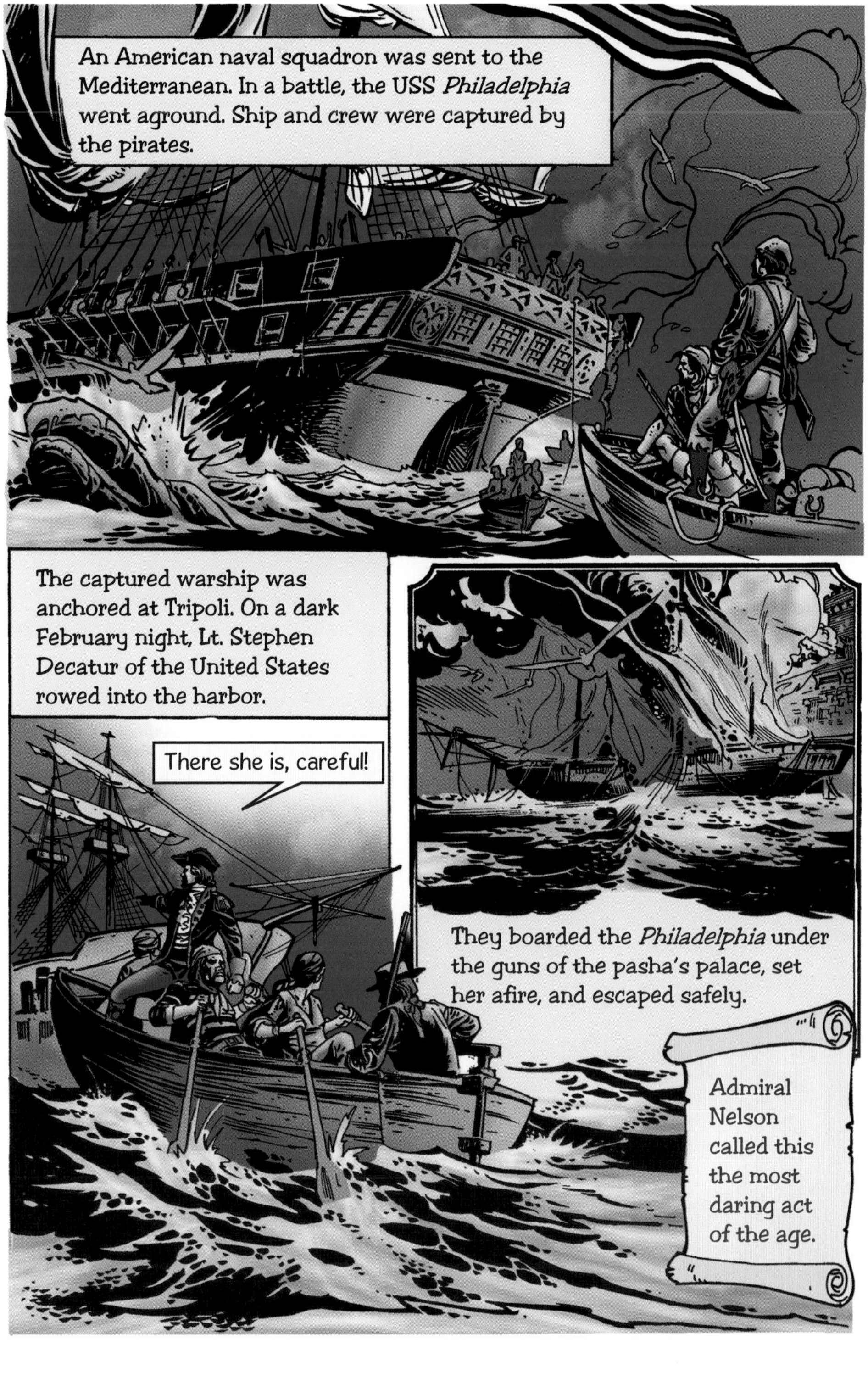
An American naval squadron was sent to the Mediterranean. In a battle, the USS *Philadelphia* went aground. Ship and crew were captured by the pirates.
The captured warship was anchored at Tripoli. On a dark February night, Lt. Stephen Decatur of the United States rowed into the harbor.
There she is, careful!
They boarded the *Philadelphia* under the guns of the pasha's palace, set her afire, and escaped safely.
Admiral Nelson called this the most daring act of the age.

10

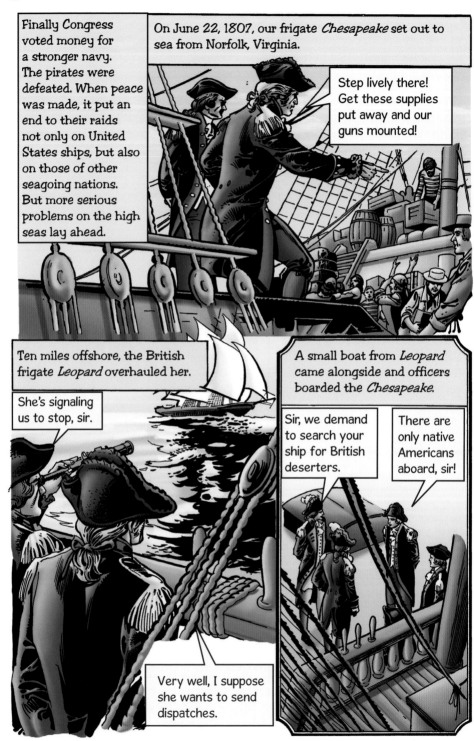

Finally Congress voted money for a stronger navy. The pirates were defeated. When peace was made, it put an end to their raids not only on United States ships, but also on those of other seagoing nations. But more serious problems on the high seas lay ahead.

On June 22, 1807, our frigate *Chesapeake* set out to sea from Norfolk, Virginia.

Step lively there! Get these supplies put away and our guns mounted!

Ten miles offshore, the British frigate *Leopard* overhauled her.

She's signaling us to stop, sir.

Very well, I suppose she wants to send dispatches.

A small boat from *Leopard* came alongside and officers boarded the *Chesapeake*.

Sir, we demand to search your ship for British deserters.

There are only native Americans aboard, sir!

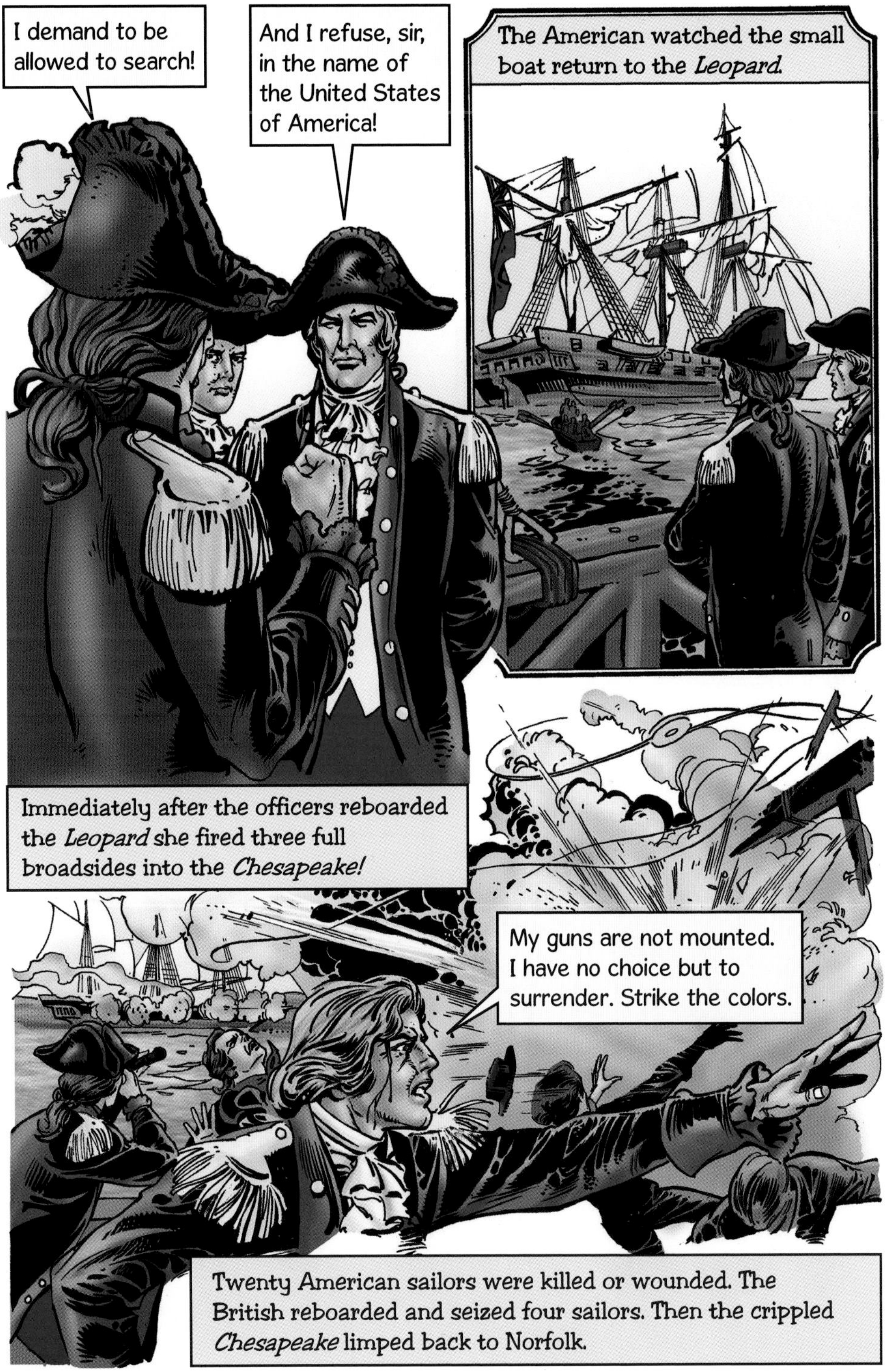
I demand to be allowed to search!
And I refuse, sir, in the name of the United States of America!
The American watched the small boat return to the *Leopard*.
Immediately after the officers reboarded the *Leopard* she fired three full broadsides into the *Chesapeake!*
My guns are not mounted. I have no choice but to surrender. Strike the colors.
Twenty American sailors were killed or wounded. The British reboarded and seized four sailors. Then the crippled *Chesapeake* limped back to Norfolk.

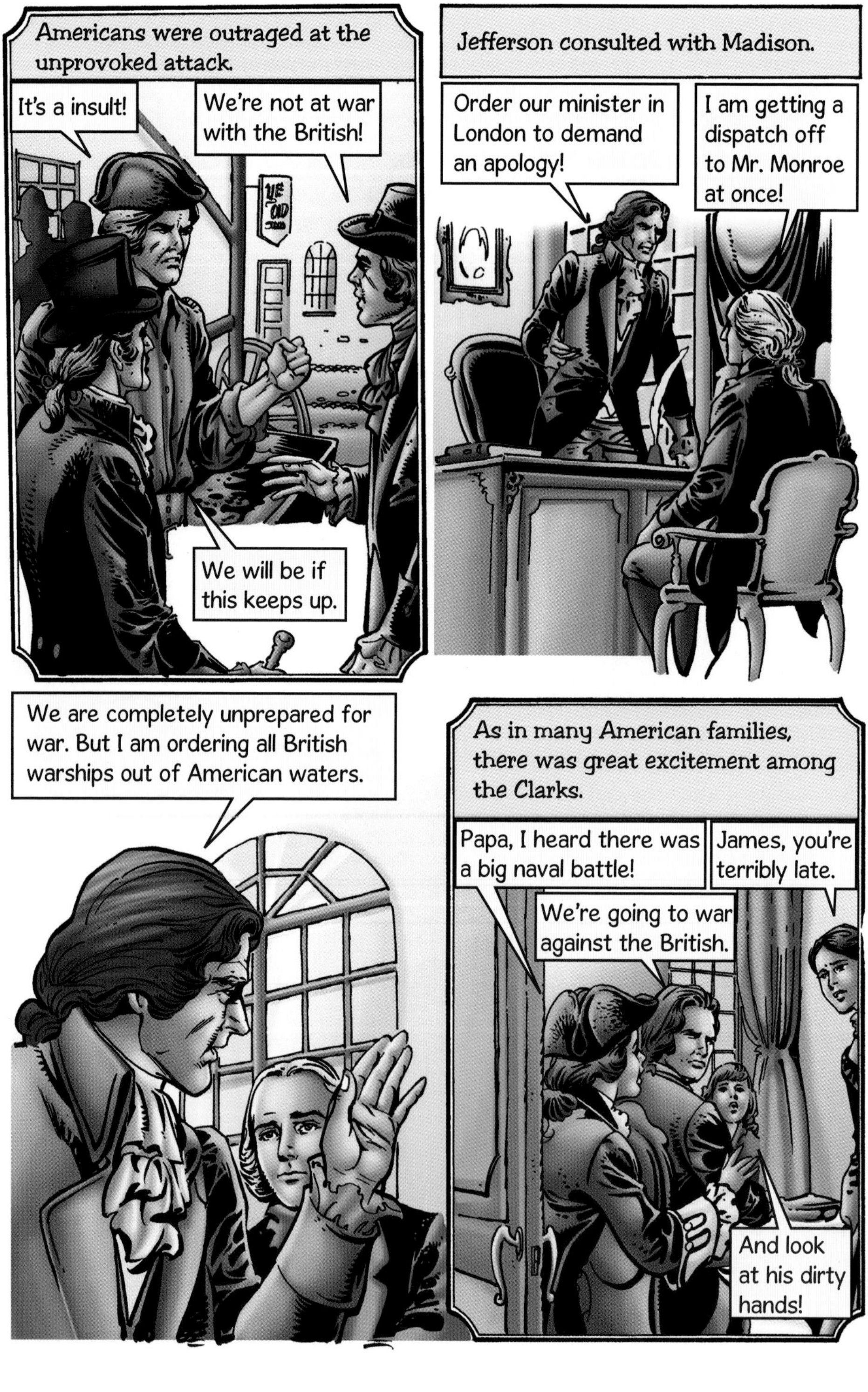

Americans were outraged at the unprovoked attack.
It's a insult!
We're not at war with the British!
YE OLD
We will be if this keeps up.
Jefferson consulted with Madison.
Order our minister in London to demand an apology!
I am getting a dispatch off to Mr. Monroe at once!
We are completely unprepared for war. But I am ordering all British warships out of American waters.
As in many American families, there was great excitement among the Clarks.
Papa, I heard there was a big naval battle!
James, you're terribly late.
We're going to war against the British.
And look at his dirty hands!

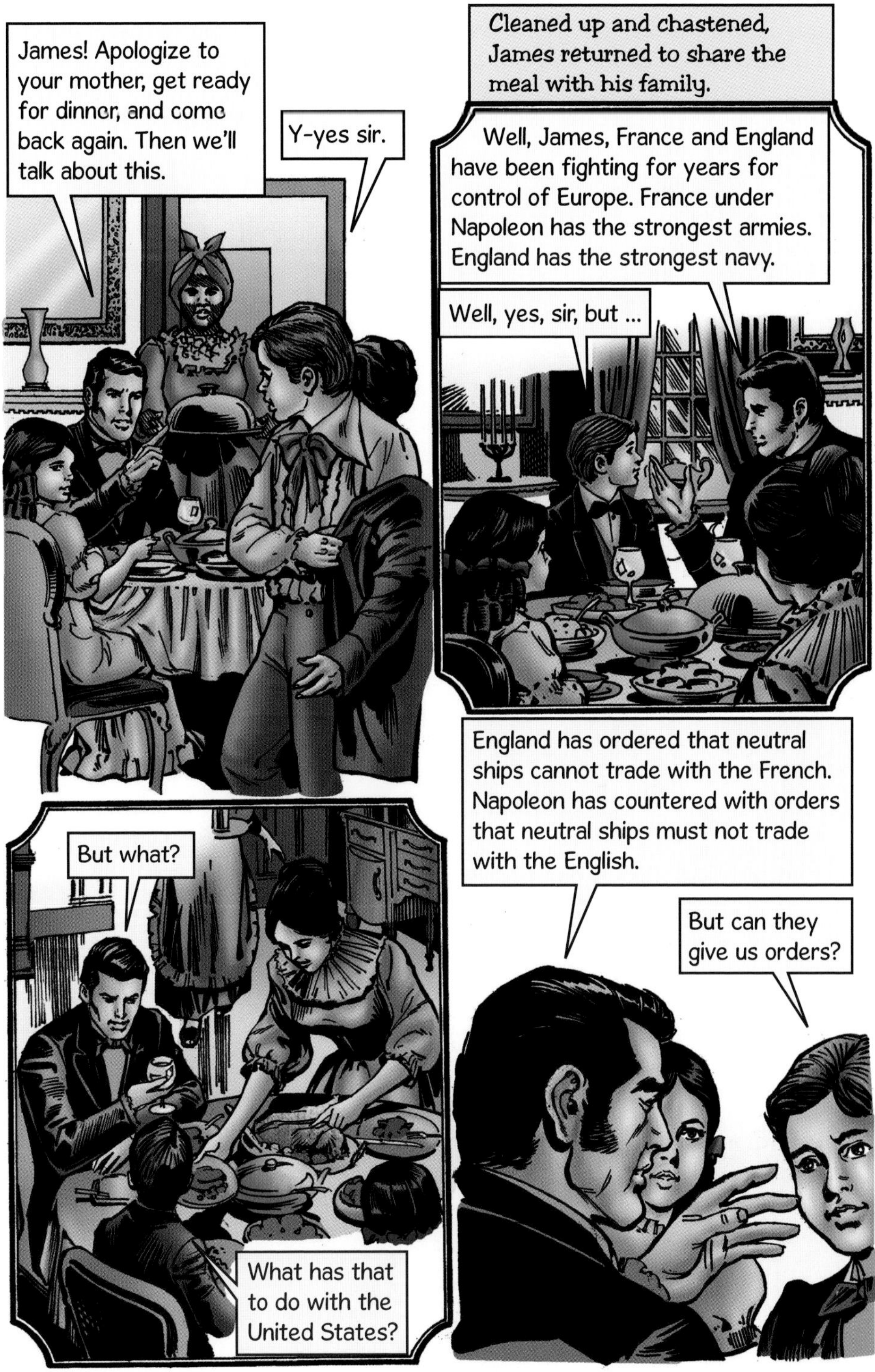
James! Apologize to your mother, get ready for dinner, and come back again. Then we'll talk about this.
Y-yes sir.
Cleaned up and chastened, James returned to share the meal with his family.
Well, James, France and England have been fighting for years for control of Europe. France under Napoleon has the strongest armies. England has the strongest navy.
Well, yes, sir, but ...
But what?
What has that to do with the United States?
England has ordered that neutral ships cannot trade with the French. Napoleon has countered with orders that neutral ships must not trade with the English.
But can they give us orders?

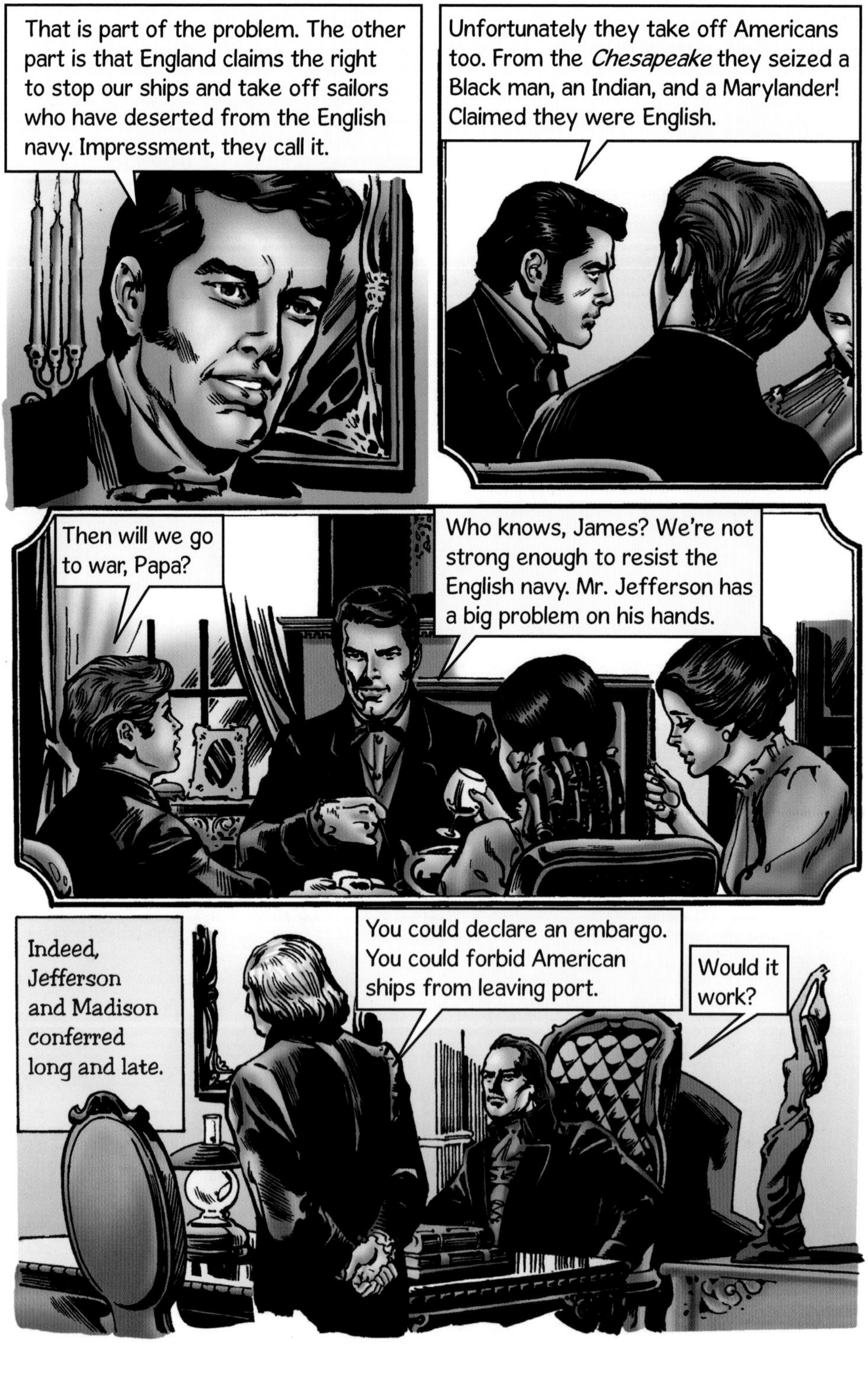
That is part of the problem. The other part is that England claims the right to stop our ships and take off sailors who have deserted from the English navy. Impressment, they call it.
Unfortunately they take off Americans too. From the *Chesapeake* they seized a Black man, an Indian, and a Marylander! Claimed they were English.
Then will we go to war, Papa?
Who knows, James? We're not strong enough to resist the English navy. Mr. Jefferson has a big problem on his hands.
Indeed, Jefferson and Madison conferred long and late.
You could declare an embargo. You could forbid American ships from leaving port.
Would it work?

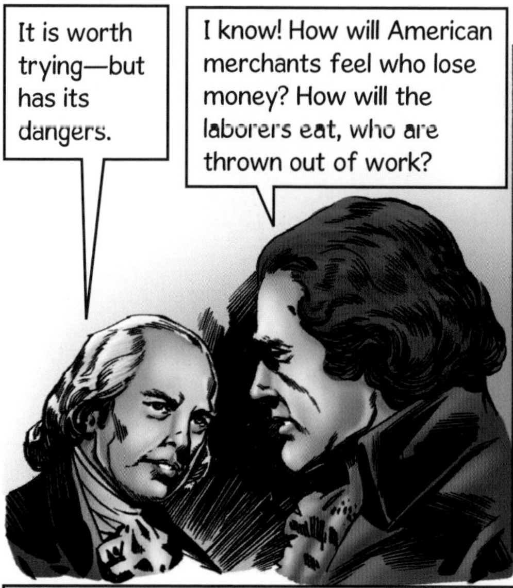
It is worth trying—but has its dangers.
I know! How will American merchants feel who lose money? How will the laborers eat, who are thrown out of work?

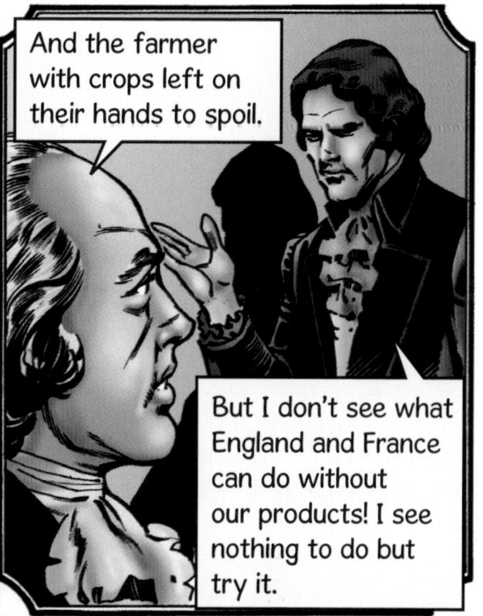
And the farmer with crops left on their hands to spoil.
But I don't see what England and France can do without our products! I see nothing to do but try it.

In 1807, Congress passed Jefferson's Embargo Act. It was a failure. It harmed the United States far more than England and France. United States trade was greatly damaged. In 1809, Congress repealed the Embargo Act. Jefferson signed the bill three days before his terms of office expired.

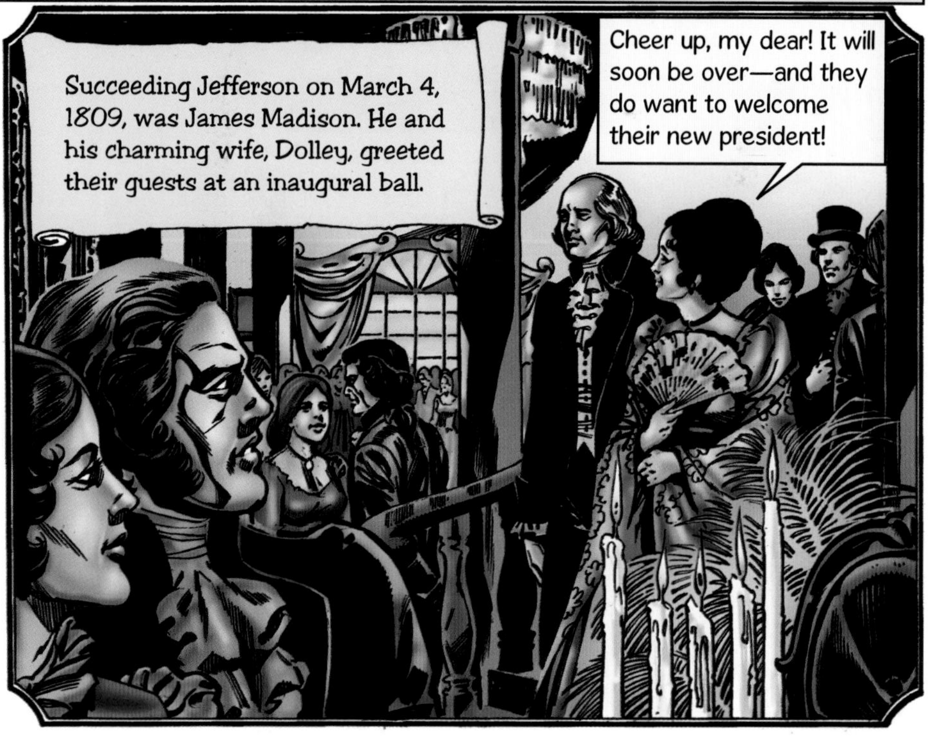
Succeeding Jefferson on March 4, 1809, was James Madison. He and his charming wife, Dolley, greeted their guests at an inaugural ball.
Cheer up, my dear! It will soon be over—and they do want to welcome their new president!

Madison was taking over Jefferson's task and his burdens. Fortunately he had Dolley to help him.

A new generation of young congressmen from the West and South are determined to fight. People are calling them the War Hawks!

Both England and France make promises, and neither keeps them. They continue to seize American ships and impress American sailors.

They are very charming and persuasive.

The War Hawks cried that British army officers and British settlers were to blame for the Native American trouble in the West. They wanted to seize Canada.

Young Henry Clay of Kentucky spoke in Congress.

I believe that the militia of Kentucky alone are competent to place upper Canada at your feet!

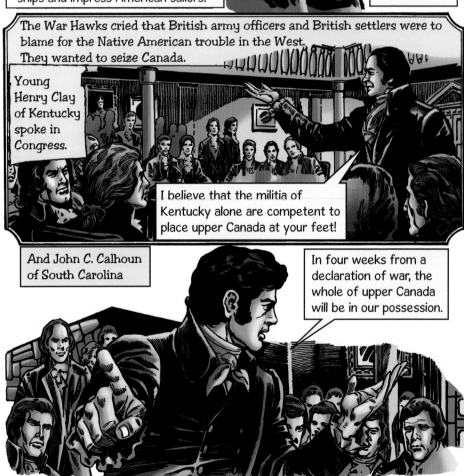

And John C. Calhoun of South Carolina

In four weeks from a declaration of war, the whole of upper Canada will be in our possession.

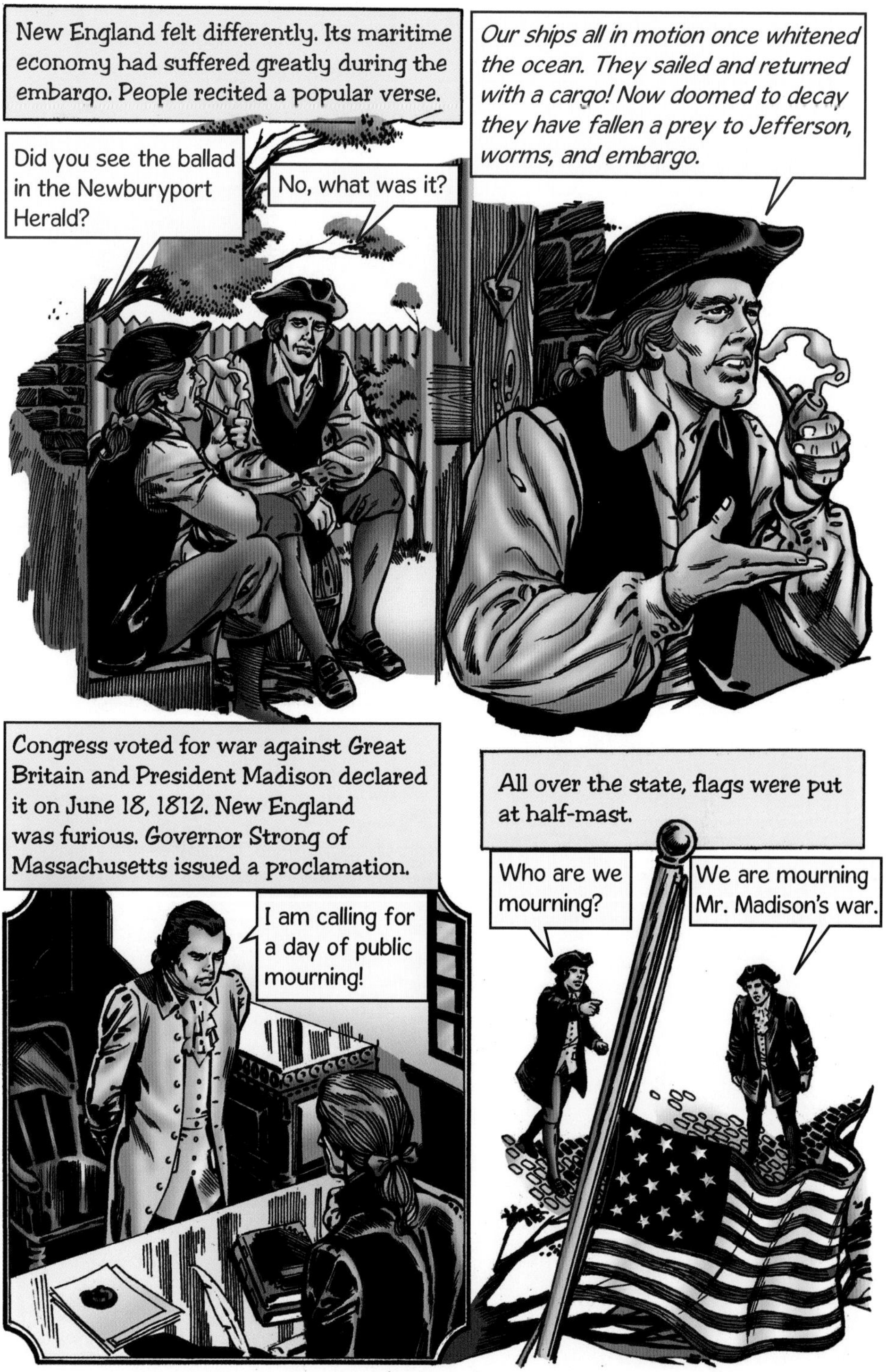
New England felt differently. Its maritime economy had suffered greatly during the embargo. People recited a popular verse.
Did you see the ballad in the Newburyport Herald?
No, what was it?
Our ships all in motion once whitened the ocean. They sailed and returned with a cargo! Now doomed to decay they have fallen a prey to Jefferson, worms, and embargo.
Congress voted for war against Great Britain and President Madison declared it on June 18, 1812. New England was furious. Governor Strong of Massachusetts issued a proclamation.
I am calling for a day of public mourning!
All over the state, flags were put at half-mast.
Who are we mourning?
We are mourning Mr. Madison's war.

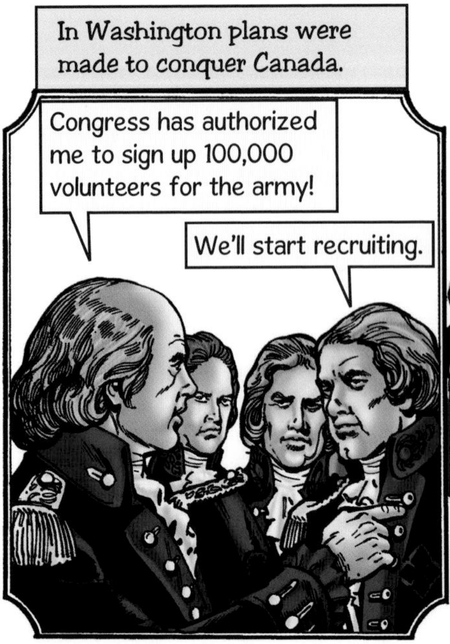
In Washington plans were made to conquer Canada.
Congress has authorized me to sign up 100,000 volunteers for the army!
We'll start recruiting.

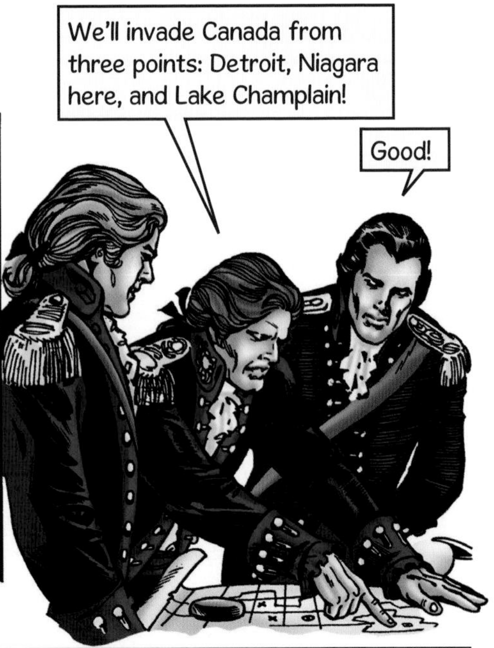
We'll invade Canada from three points: Detroit, Niagara here, and Lake Champlain!
Good!

Mackinac was a log fort on the faraway Michigan frontier. In command was young Lieutenant Hanks, U. S. Army. He was awakened suddenly one morning.

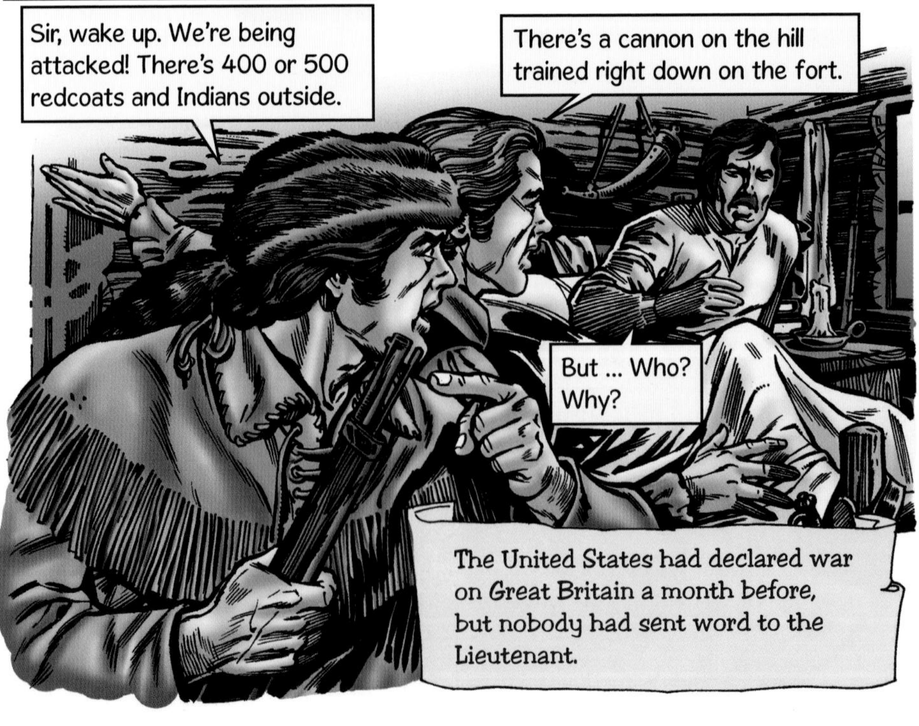
Sir, wake up. We're being attacked! There's 400 or 500 redcoats and Indians outside.
There's a cannon on the hill trained right down on the fort.
But ... Who? Why?
The United States had declared war on Great Britain a month before, but nobody had sent word to the Lieutenant.

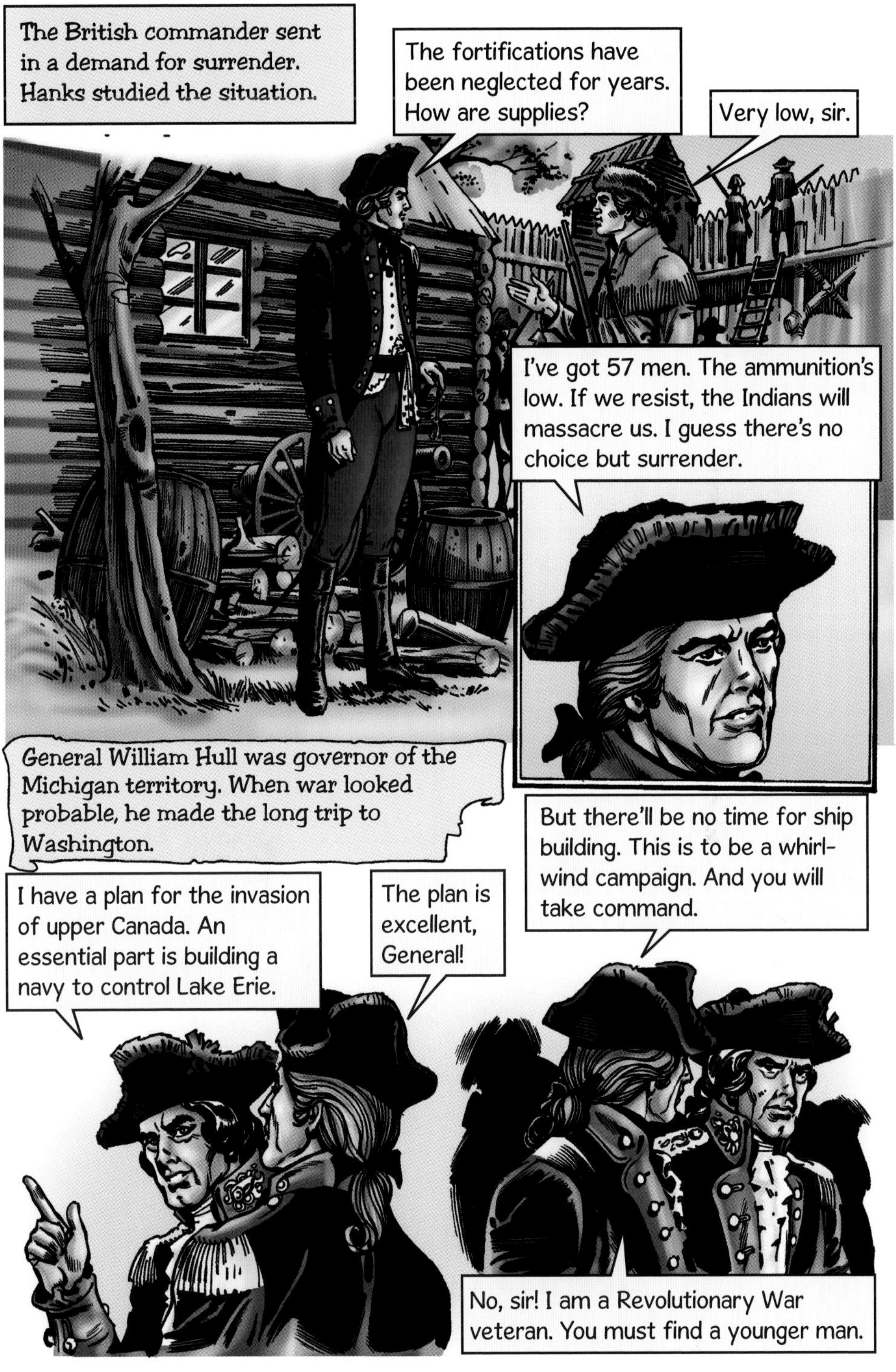
The British commander sent in a demand for surrender. Hanks studied the situation.
The fortifications have been neglected for years. How are supplies?
Very low, sir.
I've got 57 men. The ammunition's low. If we resist, the Indians will massacre us. I guess there's no choice but surrender.
General William Hull was governor of the Michigan territory. When war looked probable, he made the long trip to Washington.
I have a plan for the invasion of upper Canada. An essential part is building a navy to control Lake Erie.
The plan is excellent, General!
But there'll be no time for ship building. This is to be a whirl-wind campaign. And you will take command.
No, sir! I am a Revolutionary War veteran. You must find a younger man.

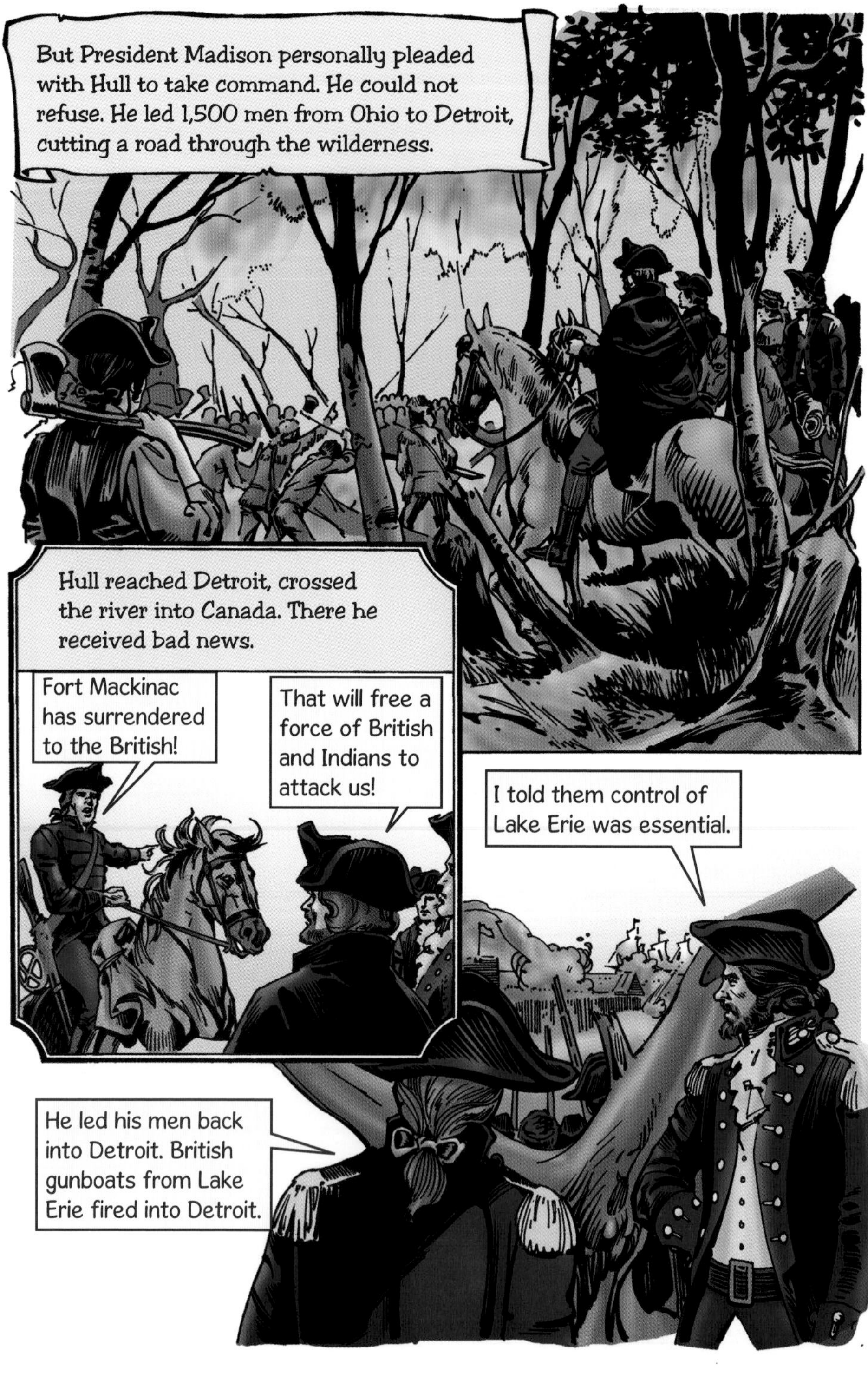
But President Madison personally pleaded with Hull to take command. He could not refuse. He led 1,500 men from Ohio to Detroit, cutting a road through the wilderness.
Hull reached Detroit, crossed the river into Canada. There he received bad news.
Fort Mackinac has surrendered to the British!
That will free a force of British and Indians to attack us!
I told them control of Lake Erie was essential.
He led his men back into Detroit. British gunboats from Lake Erie fired into Detroit.

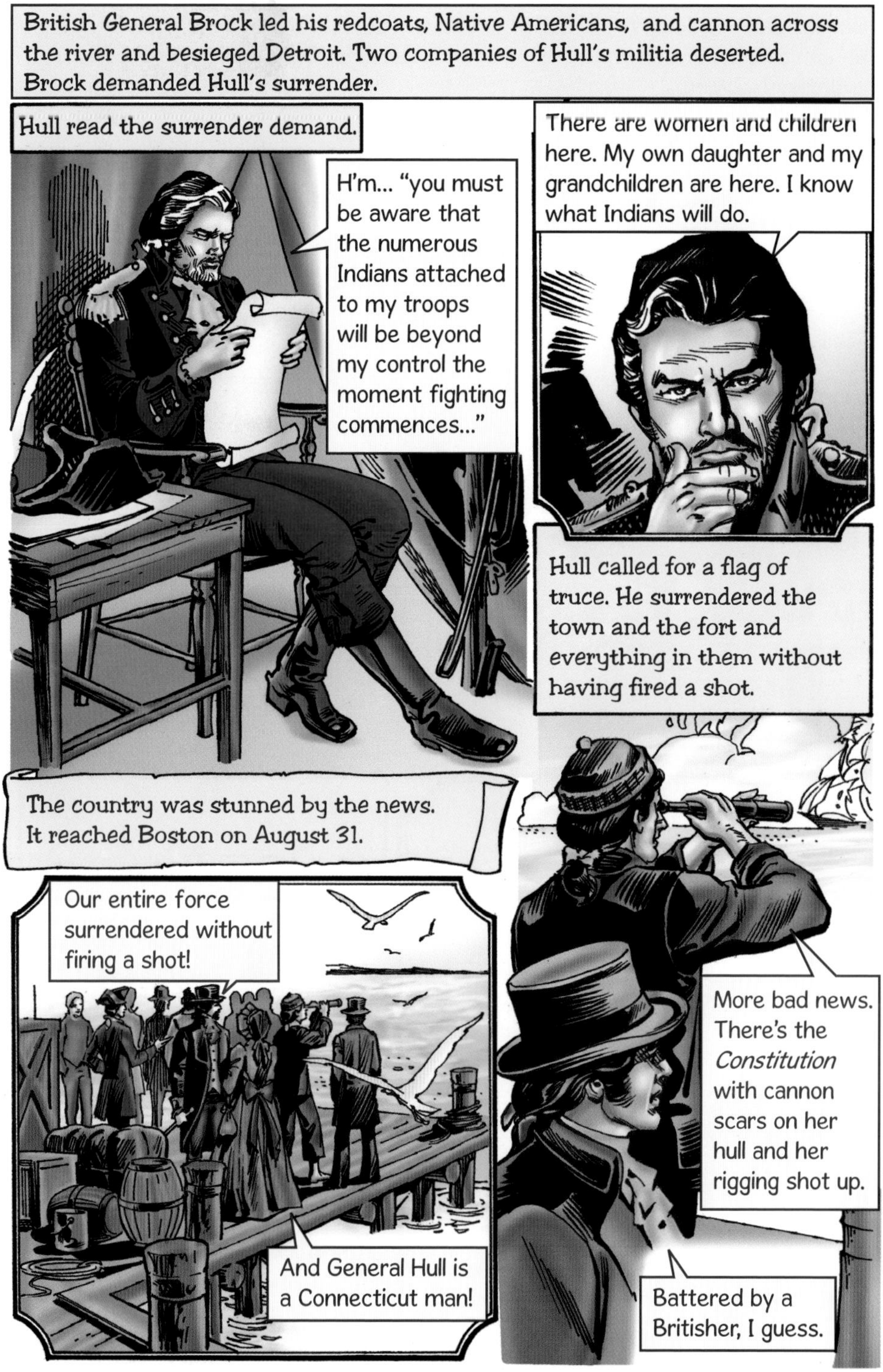
British General Brock led his redcoats, Native Americans, and cannon across the river and besieged Detroit. Two companies of Hull's militia deserted. Brock demanded Hull's surrender.
Hull read the surrender demand.
H'm... "you must be aware that the numerous Indians attached to my troops will be beyond my control the moment fighting commences..."
There are women and children here. My own daughter and my grandchildren are here. I know what Indians will do.
Hull called for a flag of truce. He surrendered the town and the fort and everything in them without having fired a shot.
The country was stunned by the news. It reached Boston on August 31.
Our entire force surrendered without firing a shot!
And General Hull is a Connecticut man!
More bad news. There's the *Constitution* with cannon scars on her hull and her rigging shot up.
Battered by a Britisher, I guess.

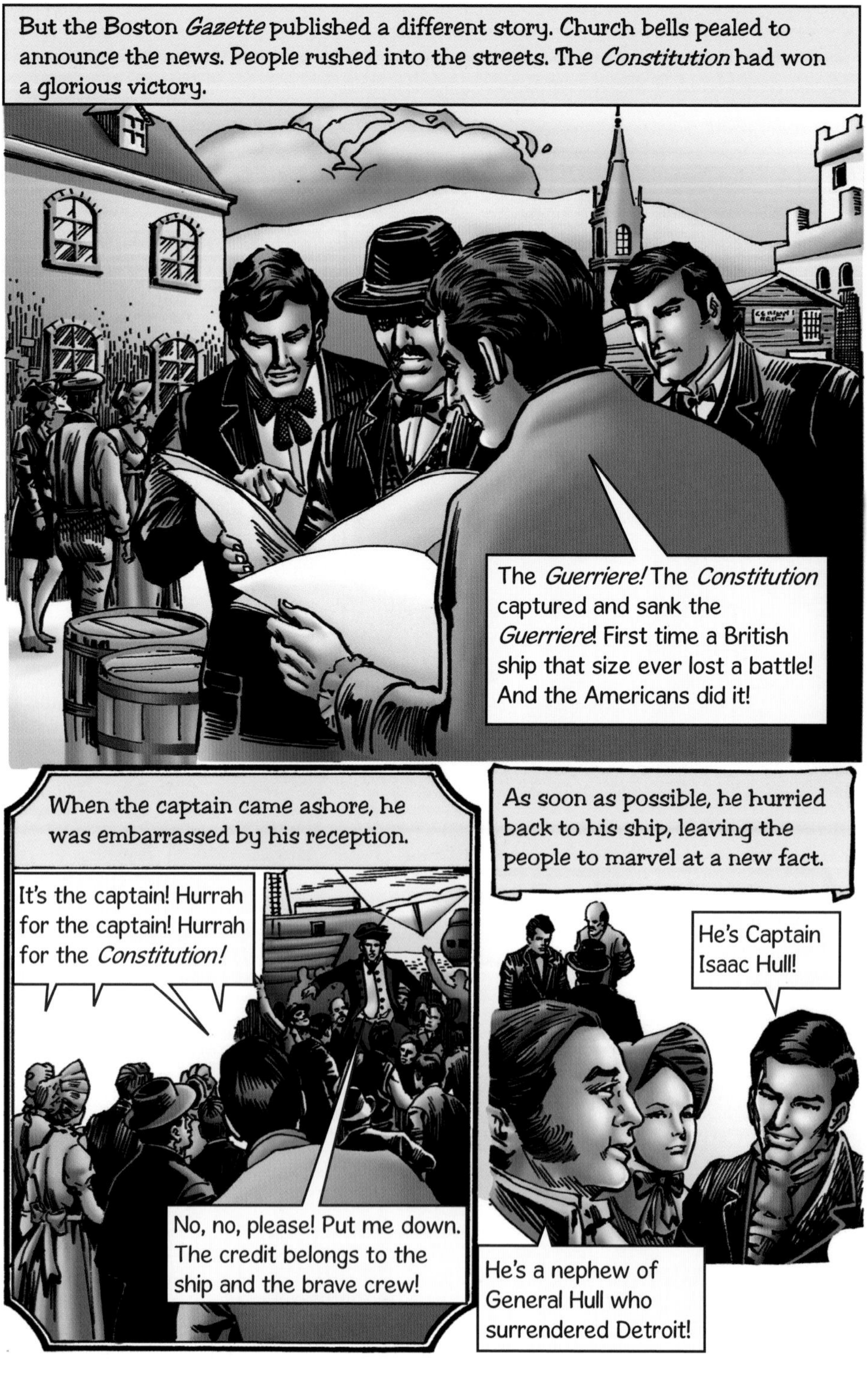
But the Boston *Gazette* published a different story. Church bells pealed to announce the news. People rushed into the streets. The *Constitution* had won a glorious victory.
The *Guerriere!* The *Constitution* captured and sank the *Guerriere*! First time a British ship that size ever lost a battle! And the Americans did it!
When the captain came ashore, he was embarrassed by his reception.
It's the captain! Hurrah for the captain! Hurrah for the *Constitution!*
No, no, please! Put me down. The credit belongs to the ship and the brave crew!
As soon as possible, he hurried back to his ship, leaving the people to marvel at a new fact.
He's Captain Isaac Hull!
He's a nephew of General Hull who surrendered Detroit!

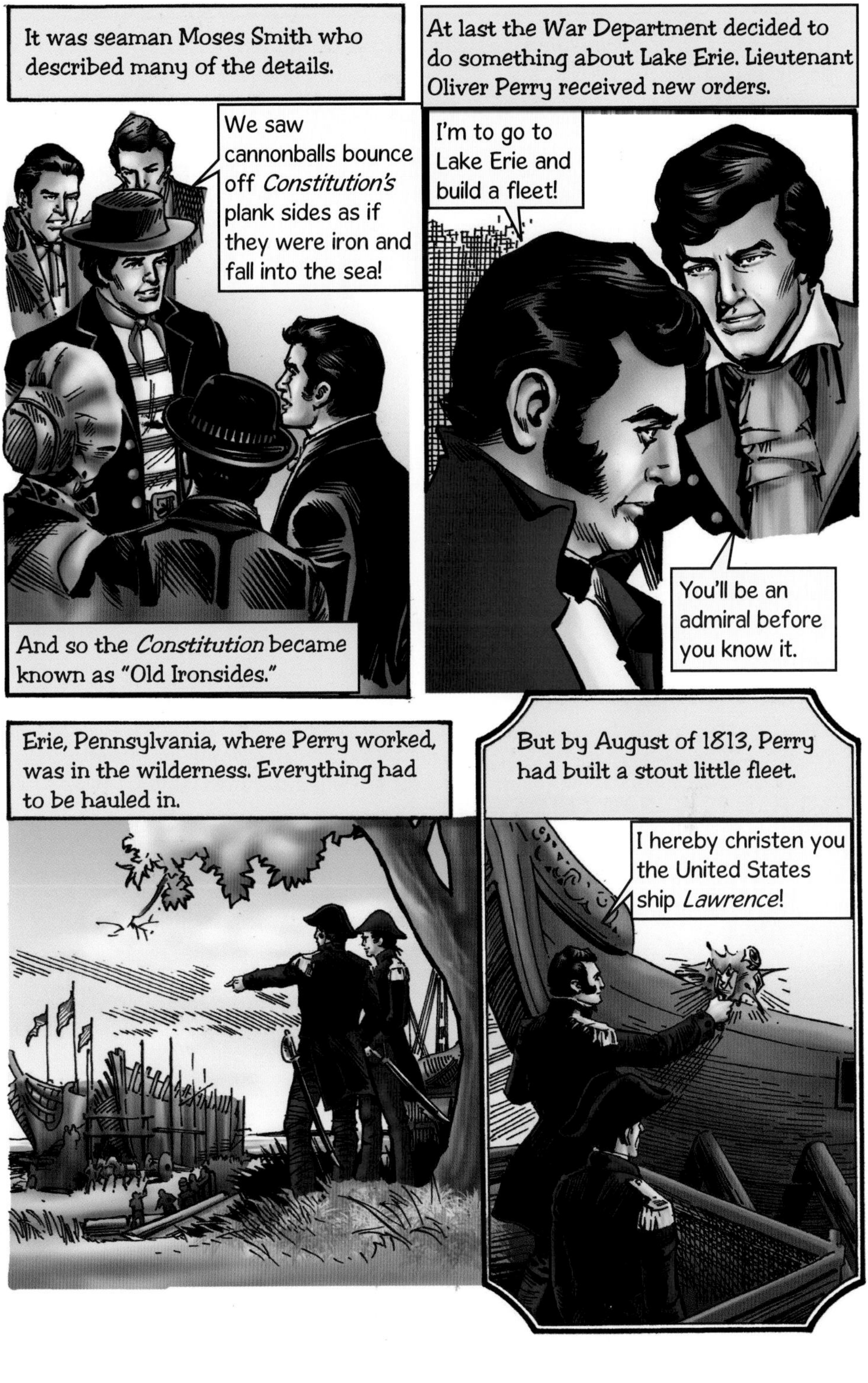
It was seaman Moses Smith who described many of the details.
We saw cannonballs bounce off *Constitution's* plank sides as if they were iron and fall into the sea!
And so the *Constitution* became known as "Old Ironsides."
At last the War Department decided to do something about Lake Erie. Lieutenant Oliver Perry received new orders.
I'm to go to Lake Erie and build a fleet!
You'll be an admiral before you know it.
Erie, Pennsylvania, where Perry worked, was in the wilderness. Everything had to be hauled in.
But by August of 1813, Perry had built a stout little fleet.
I hereby christen you the United States ship *Lawrence*!

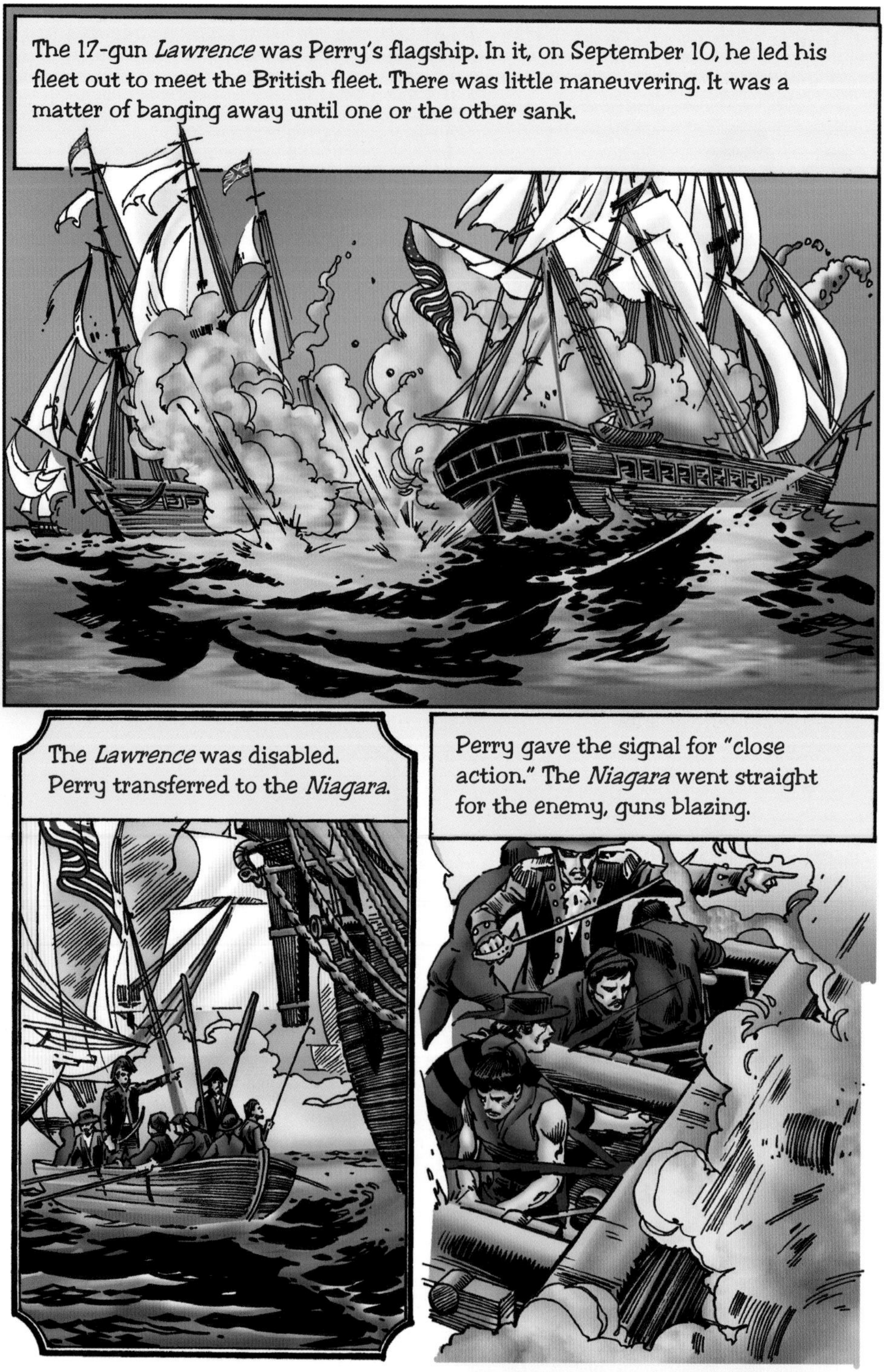
The 17-gun *Lawrence* was Perry's flagship. In it, on September 10, he led his fleet out to meet the British fleet. There was little maneuvering. It was a matter of banging away until one or the other sank.
The *Lawrence* was disabled. Perry transferred to the *Niagara*.
Perry gave the signal for "close action." The *Niagara* went straight for the enemy, guns blazing.

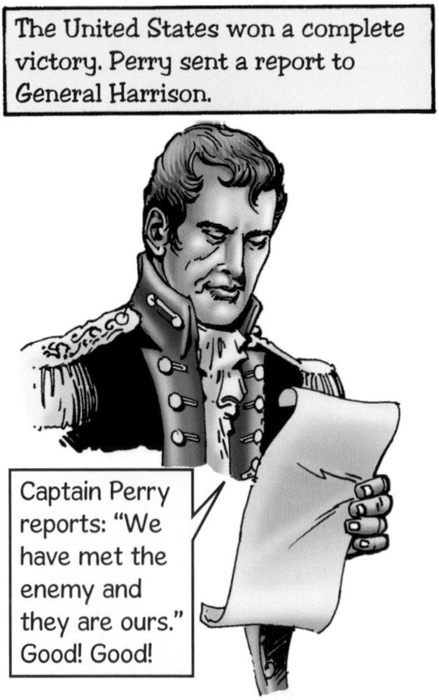
The United States won a complete victory. Perry sent a report to General Harrison.
Captain Perry reports: "We have met the enemy and they are ours." Good! Good!

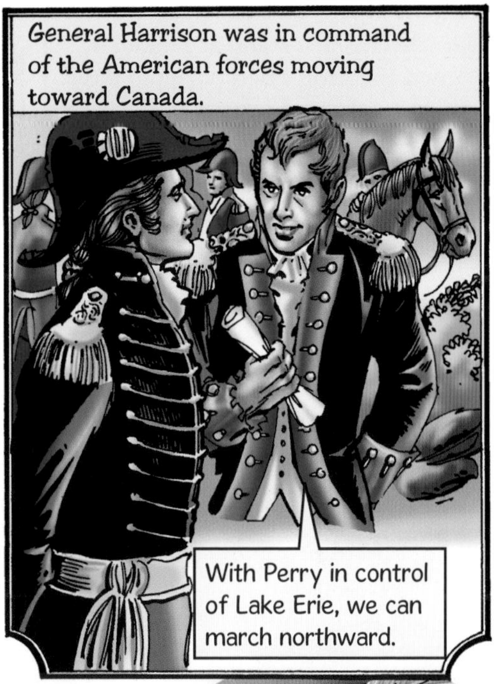
General Harrison was in command of the American forces moving toward Canada.
With Perry in control of Lake Erie, we can march northward.

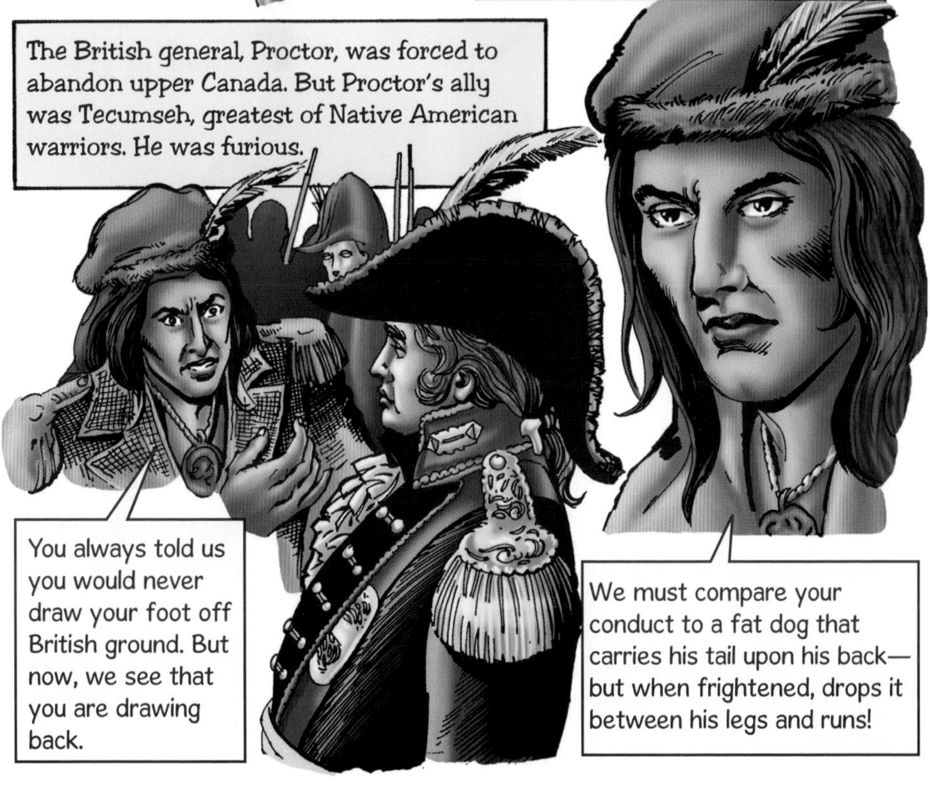
The British general, Proctor, was forced to abandon upper Canada. But Proctor's ally was Tecumseh, greatest of Native American warriors. He was furious.
You always told us you would never draw your foot off British ground. But now, we see that you are drawing back.
We must compare your conduct to a fat dog that carries his tail upon his back—but when frightened, drops it between his legs and runs!

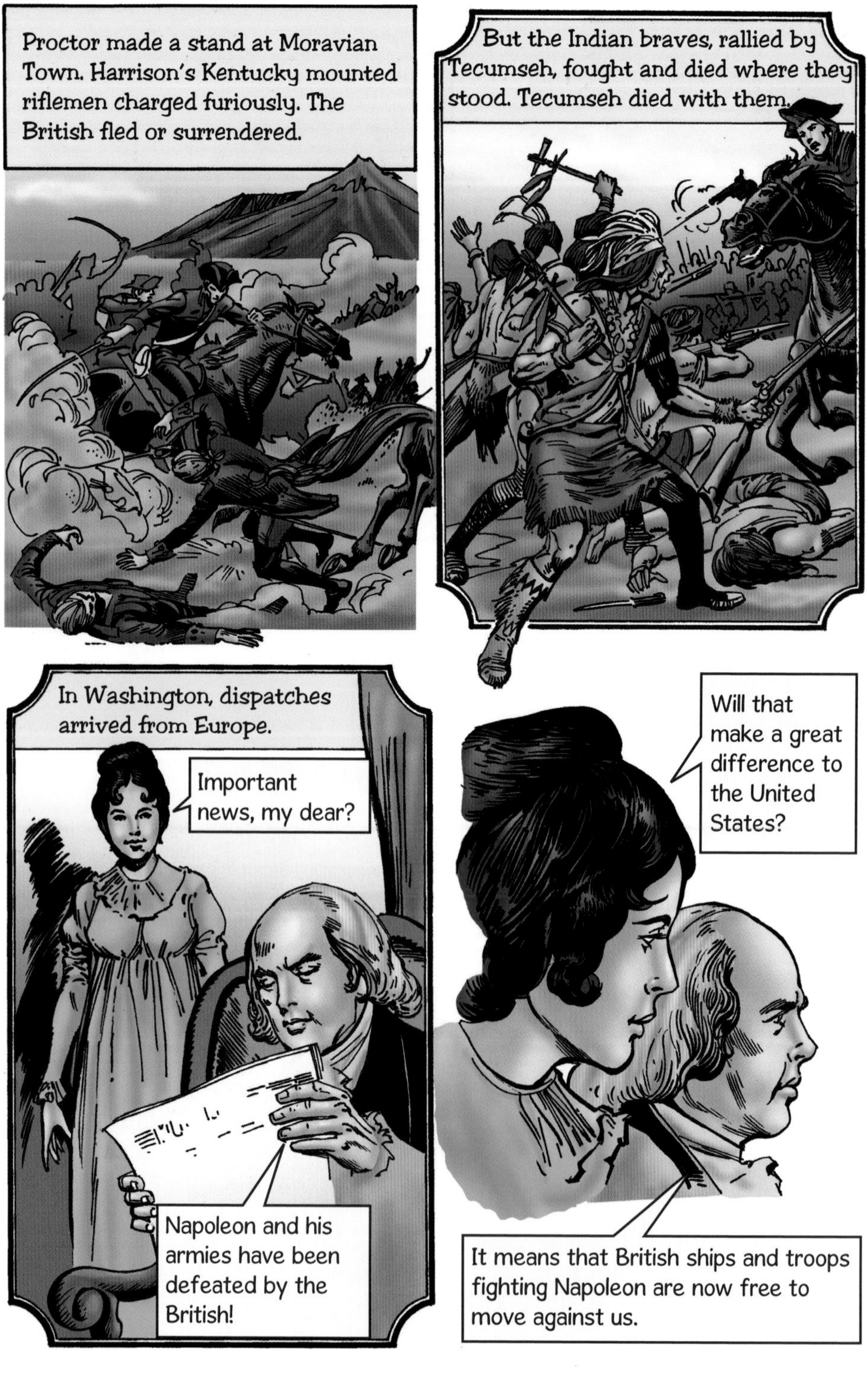
Proctor made a stand at Moravian Town. Harrison's Kentucky mounted riflemen charged furiously. The British fled or surrendered.
But the Indian braves, rallied by Tecumseh, fought and died where they stood. Tecumseh died with them.
In Washington, dispatches arrived from Europe.
Important news, my dear?
Napoleon and his armies have been defeated by the British!
Will that make a great difference to the United States?
It means that British ships and troops fighting Napoleon are now free to move against us.

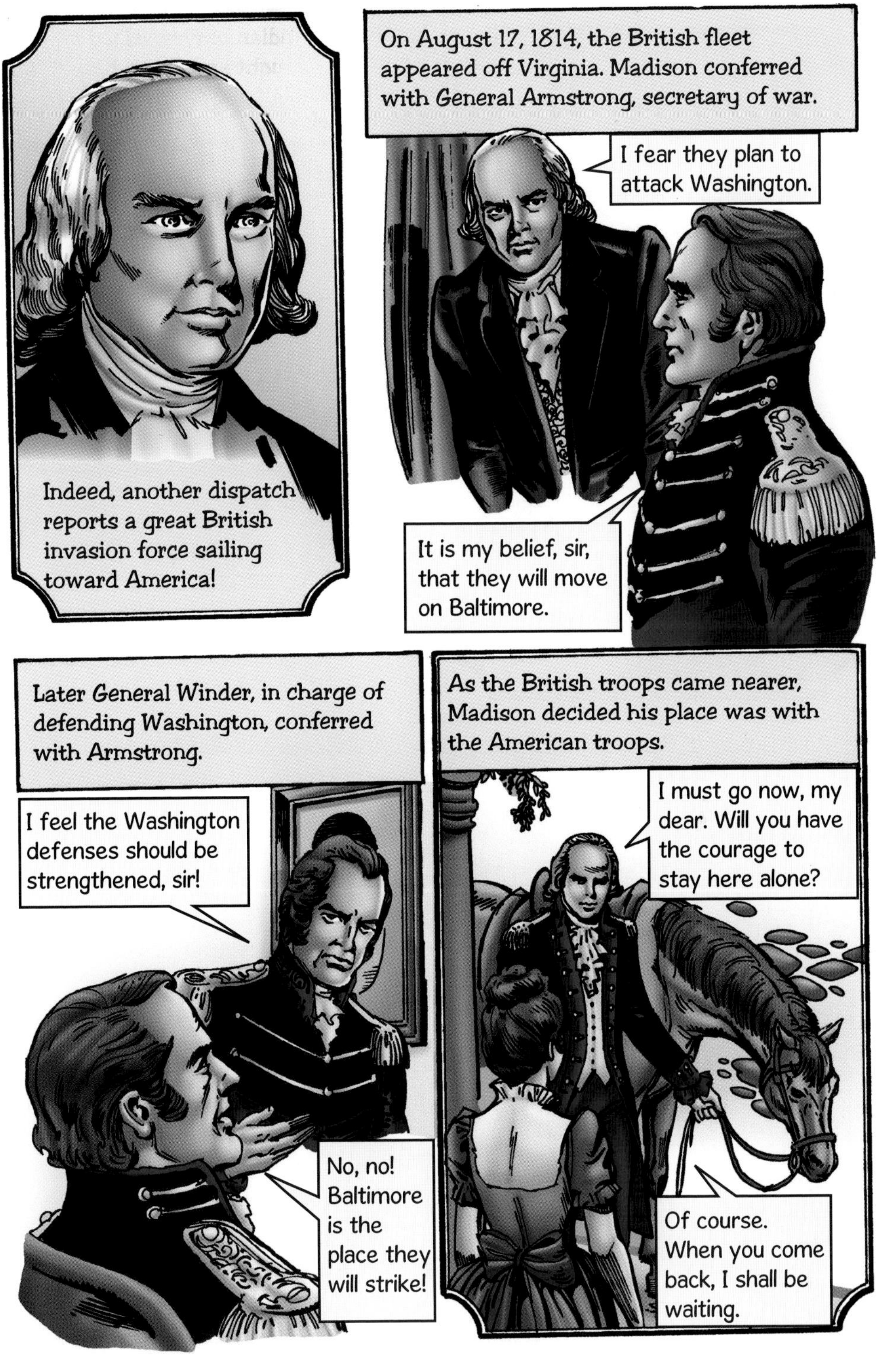
Indeed, another dispatch reports a great British invasion force sailing toward America!
On August 17, 1814, the British fleet appeared off Virginia. Madison conferred with General Armstrong, secretary of war.
I fear they plan to attack Washington.
It is my belief, sir, that they will move on Baltimore.
Later General Winder, in charge of defending Washington, conferred with Armstrong.
I feel the Washington defenses should be strengthened, sir!
No, no! Baltimore is the place they will strike!
As the British troops came nearer, Madison decided his place was with the American troops.
I must go now, my dear. Will you have the courage to stay here alone?
Of course. When you come back, I shall be waiting.

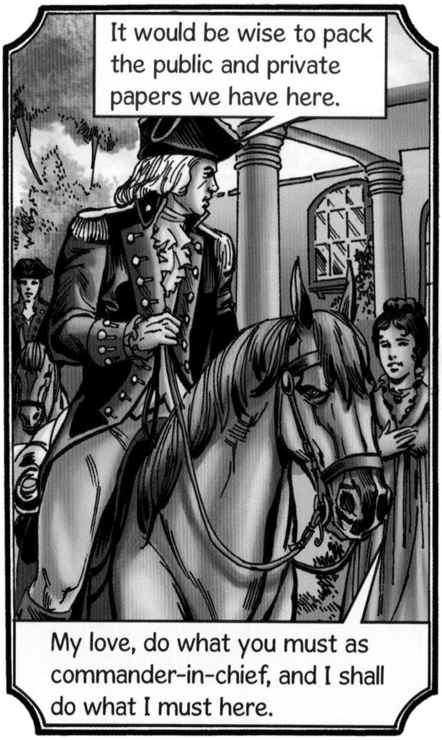
It would be wise to pack the public and private papers we have here.
My love, do what you must as commander-in-chief, and I shall do what I must here.

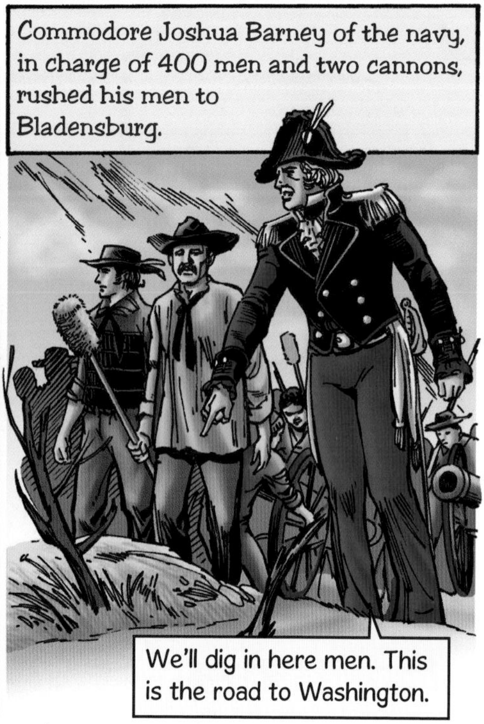
Commodore Joshua Barney of the navy, in charge of 400 men and two cannons, rushed his men to Bladensburg.
We'll dig in here men. This is the road to Washington.

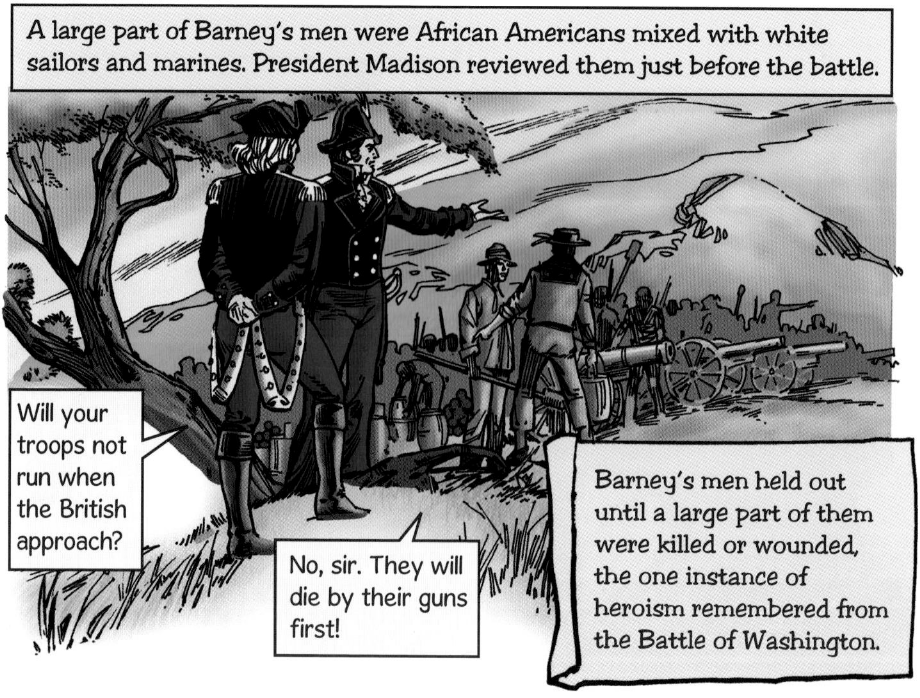
A large part of Barney's men were African Americans mixed with white sailors and marines. President Madison reviewed them just before the battle.
Will your troops not run when the British approach?
No, sir. They will die by their guns first!
Barney's men held out until a large part of them were killed or wounded, the one instance of heroism remembered from the Battle of Washington.

The large body of militiamen defending Washington, mostly untrained and poorly positioned by General Armstrong, broke and ran under the British attack. Many never fired their guns.

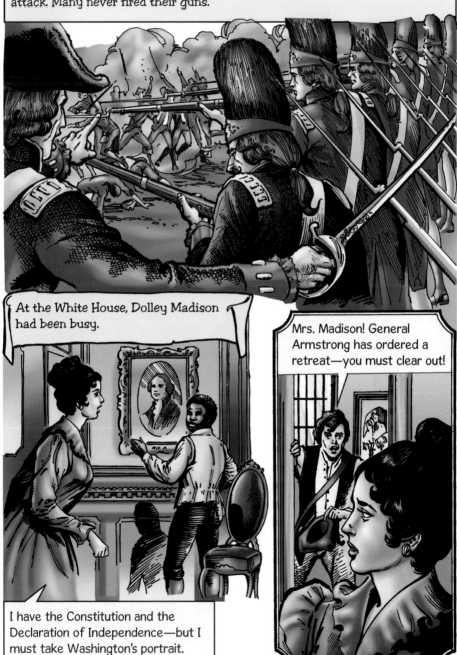

At the White House, Dolley Madison had been busy.

I have the Constitution and the Declaration of Independence—but I must take Washington's portrait.

Mrs. Madison! General Armstrong has ordered a retreat—you must clear out!

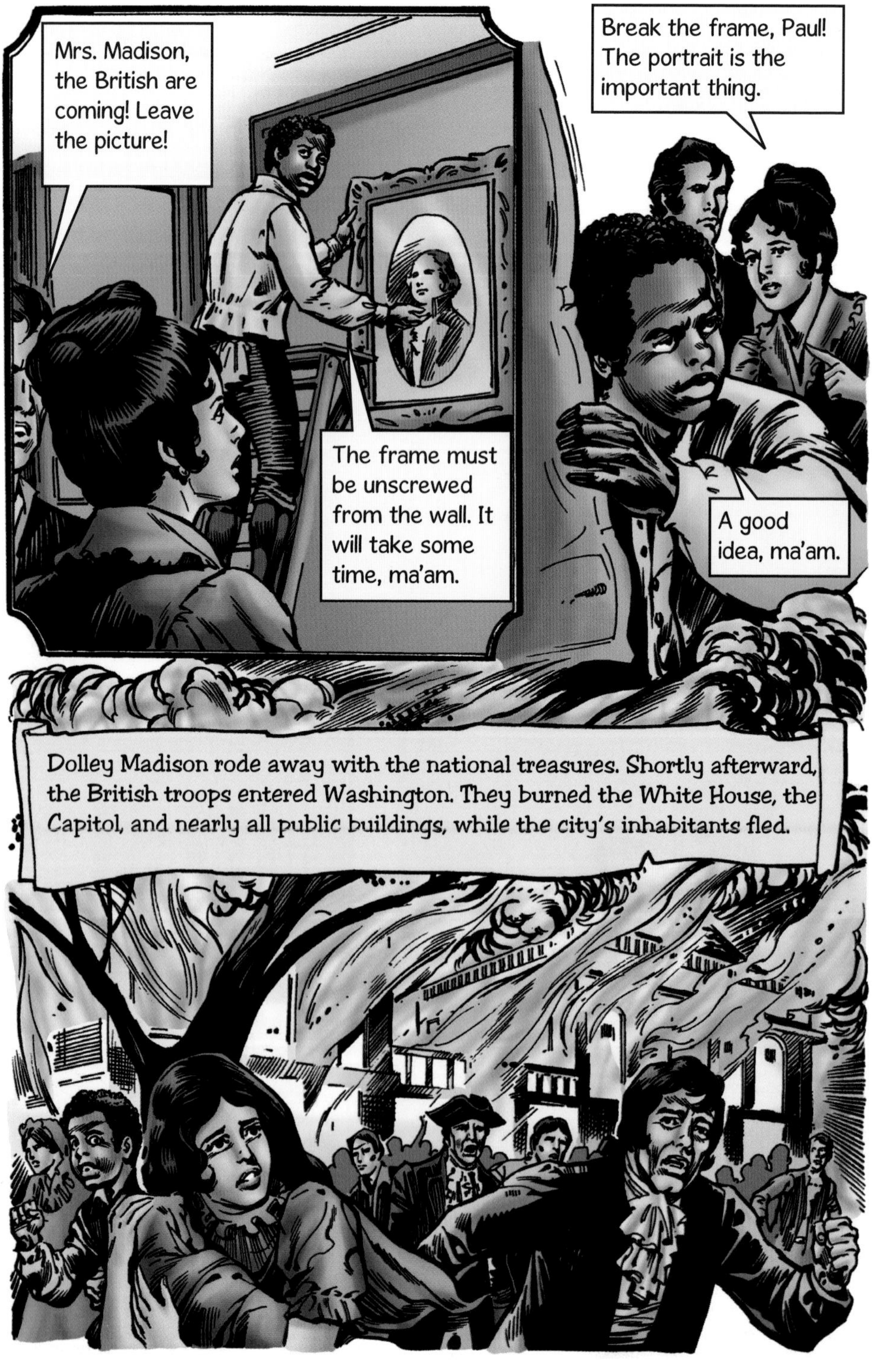
Mrs. Madison, the British are coming! Leave the picture!
The frame must be unscrewed from the wall. It will take some time, ma'am.
Break the frame, Paul! The portrait is the important thing.
A good idea, ma'am.
Dolley Madison rode away with the national treasures. Shortly afterward, the British troops entered Washington. They burned the White House, the Capitol, and nearly all public buildings, while the city's inhabitants fled.

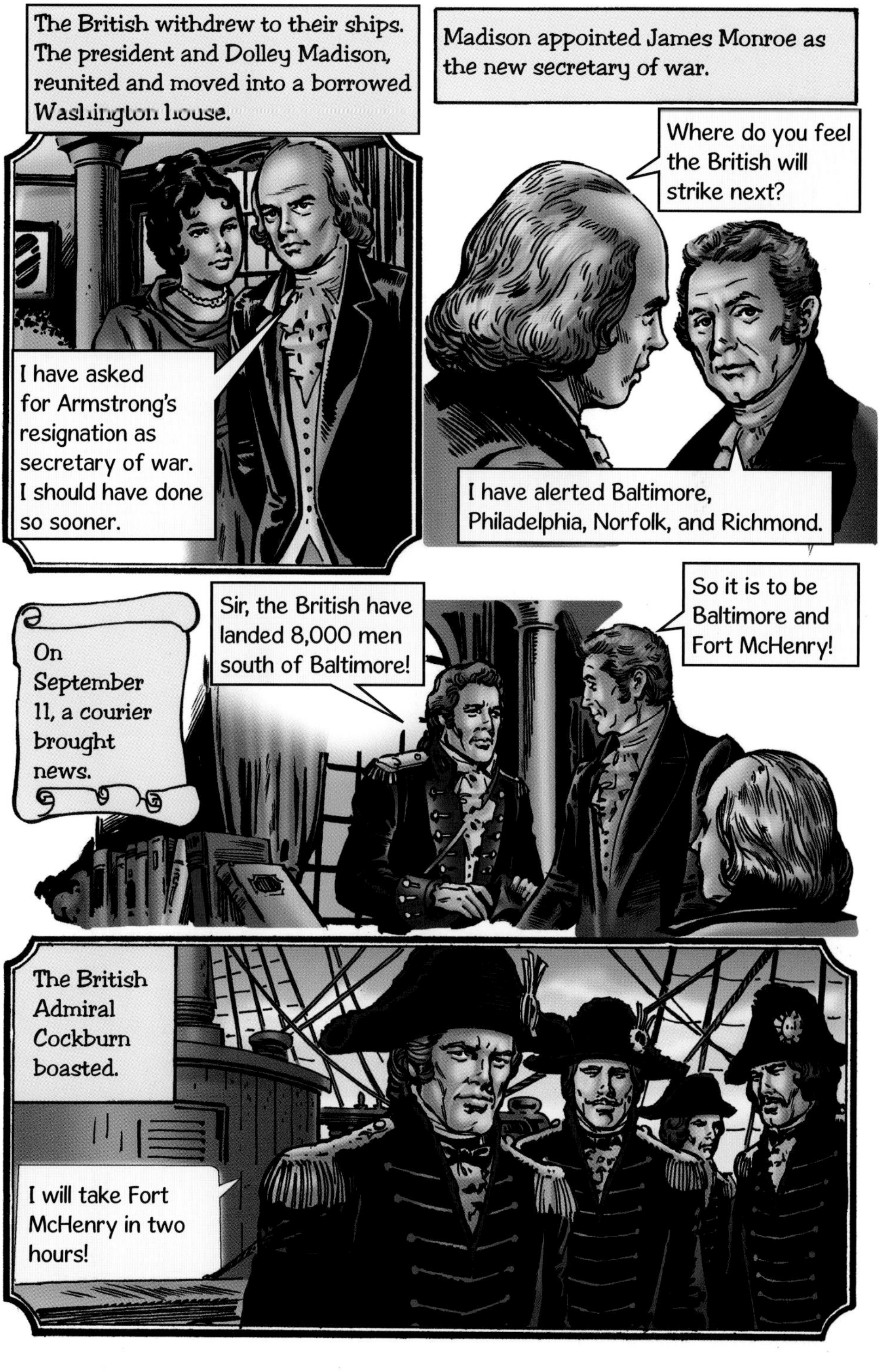
The British withdrew to their ships. The president and Dolley Madison, reunited and moved into a borrowed Washington house.
I have asked for Armstrong's resignation as secretary of war. I should have done so sooner.
Madison appointed James Monroe as the new secretary of war.
Where do you feel the British will strike next?
I have alerted Baltimore, Philadelphia, Norfolk, and Richmond.
On September 11, a courier brought news.
Sir, the British have landed 8,000 men south of Baltimore!
So it is to be Baltimore and Fort McHenry!
The British Admiral Cockburn boasted.
I will take Fort McHenry in two hours!

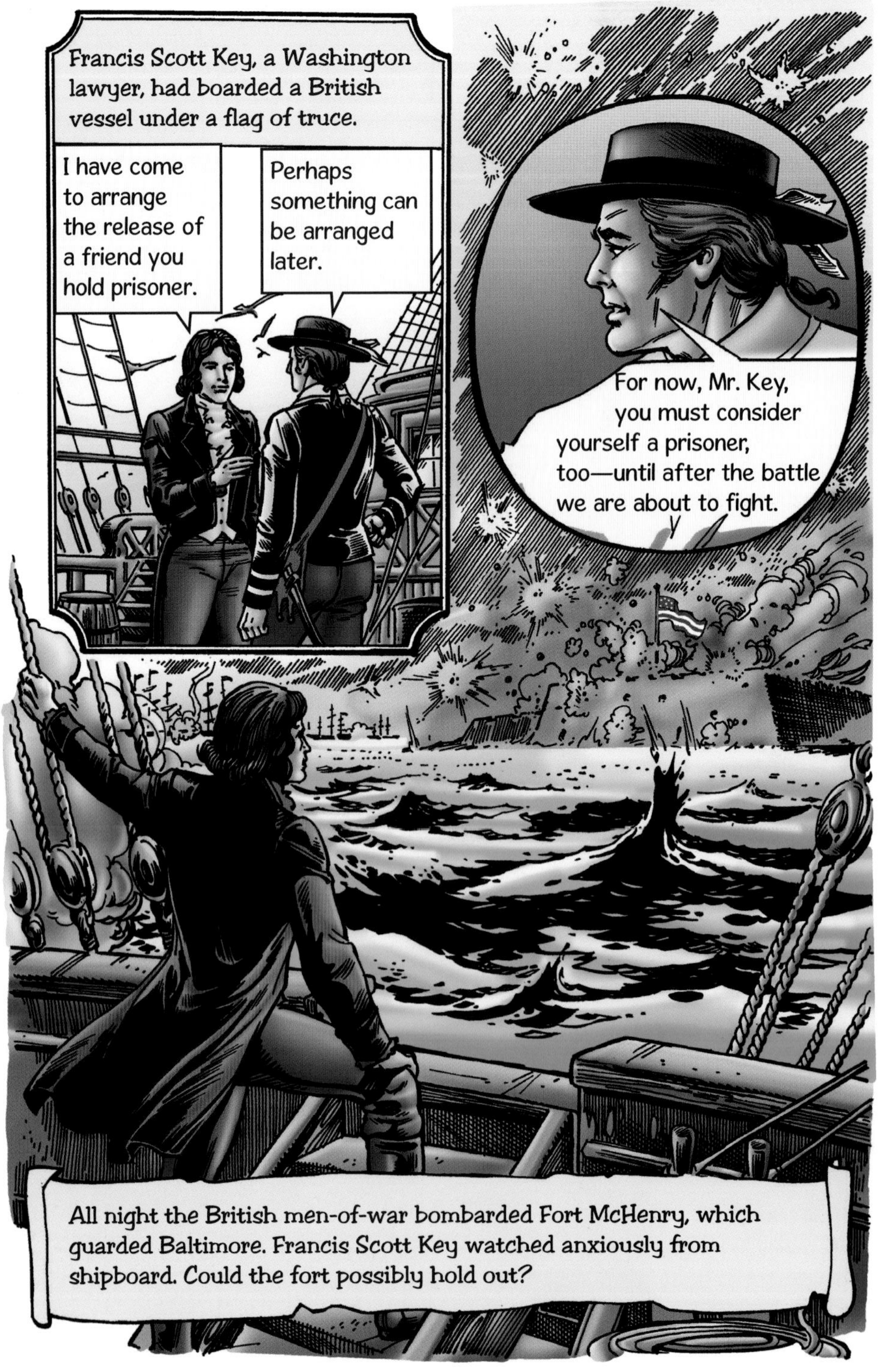
Francis Scott Key, a Washington lawyer, had boarded a British vessel under a flag of truce.
I have come to arrange the release of a friend you hold prisoner.
Perhaps something can be arranged later.
For now, Mr. Key, you must consider yourself a prisoner, too—until after the battle we are about to fight.
All night the British men-of-war bombarded Fort McHenry, which guarded Baltimore. Francis Scott Key watched anxiously from shipboard. Could the fort possibly hold out?

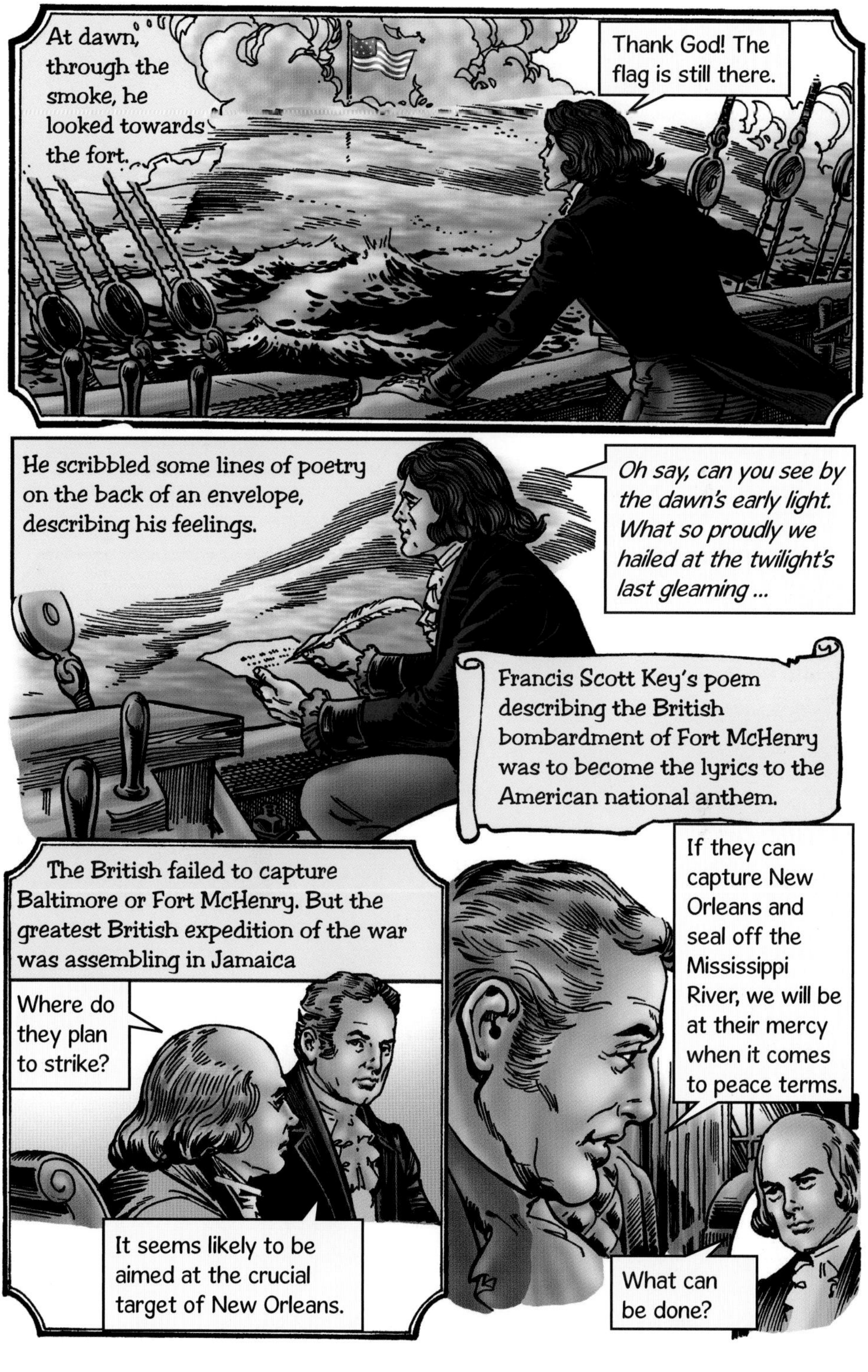
At dawn, through the smoke, he looked towards the fort.
Thank God! The flag is still there.
He scribbled some lines of poetry on the back of an envelope, describing his feelings.
Oh say, can you see by the dawn's early light. What so proudly we hailed at the twilight's last gleaming ...
Francis Scott Key's poem describing the British bombardment of Fort McHenry was to become the lyrics to the American national anthem.
The British failed to capture Baltimore or Fort McHenry. But the greatest British expedition of the war was assembling in Jamaica
Where do they plan to strike?
It seems likely to be aimed at the crucial target of New Orleans.
If they can capture New Orleans and seal off the Mississippi River, we will be at their mercy when it comes to peace terms.
What can be done?

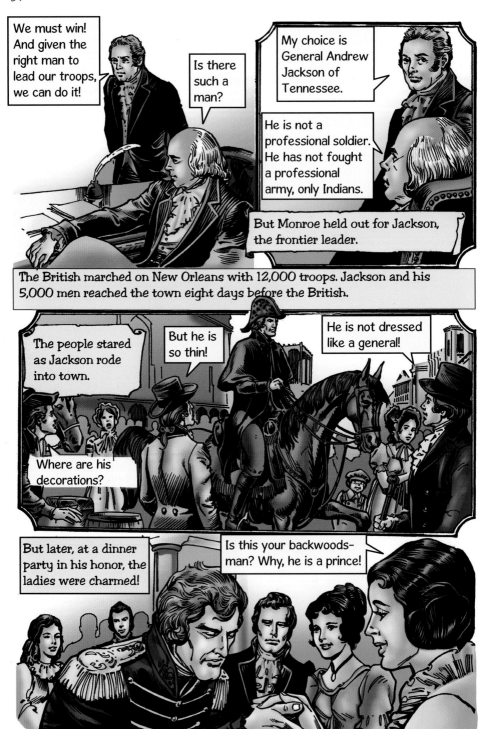

We must win! And given the right man to lead our troops, we can do it!

Is there such a man?

My choice is General Andrew Jackson of Tennessee.

He is not a professional soldier. He has not fought a professional army, only Indians.

But Monroe held out for Jackson, the frontier leader.

The British marched on New Orleans with 12,000 troops. Jackson and his 5,000 men reached the town eight days before the British.

The people stared as Jackson rode into town.

But he is so thin!

He is not dressed like a general!

Where are his decorations?

But later, at a dinner party in his honor, the ladies were charmed!

Is this your backwoodsman? Why, he is a prince!

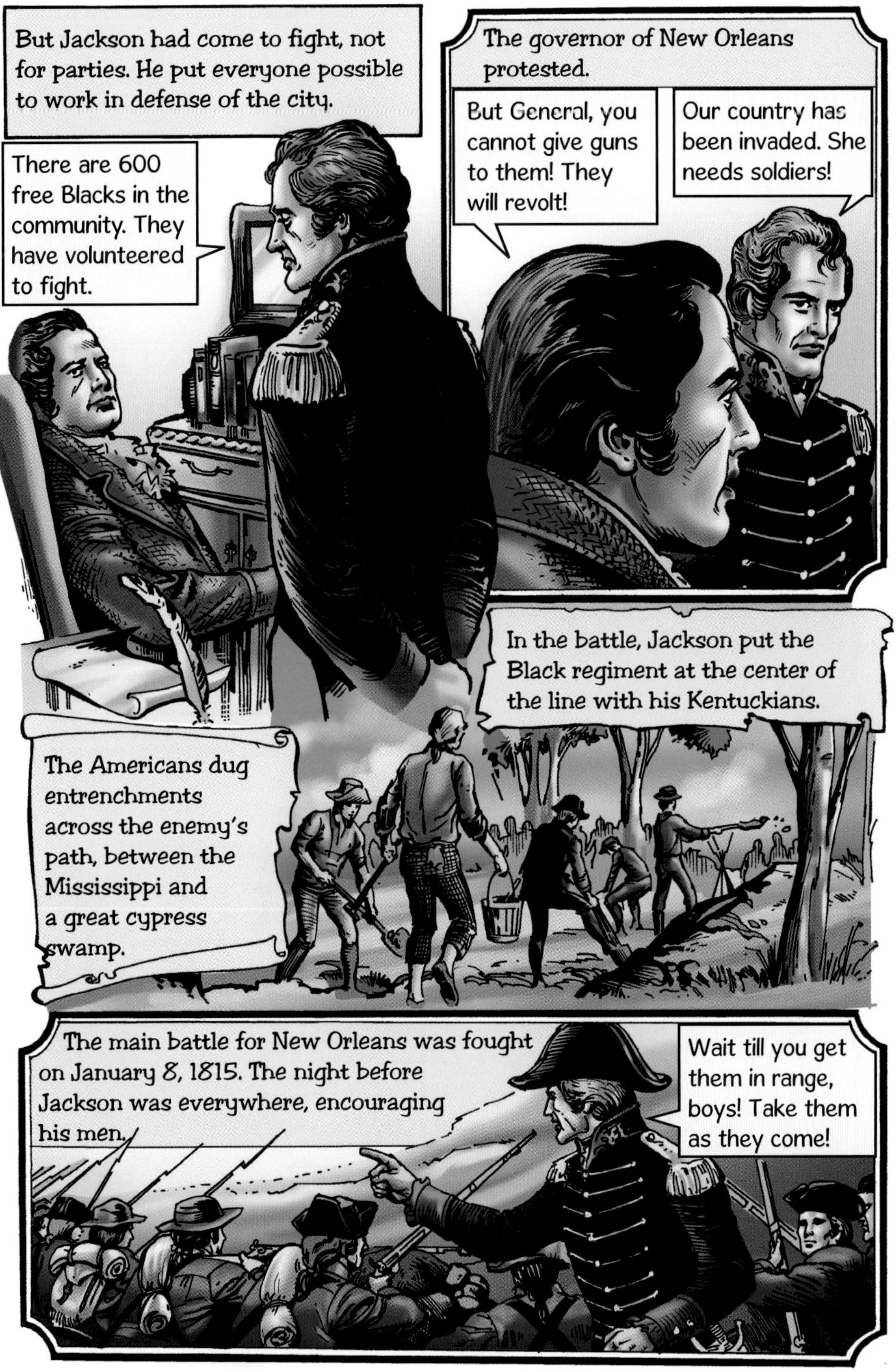
But Jackson had come to fight, not for parties. He put everyone possible to work in defense of the city.
There are 600 free Blacks in the community. They have volunteered to fight.
The governor of New Orleans protested.
But General, you cannot give guns to them! They will revolt!
Our country has been invaded. She needs soldiers!
In the battle, Jackson put the Black regiment at the center of the line with his Kentuckians.
The Americans dug entrenchments across the enemy's path, between the Mississippi and a great cypress swamp.
The main battle for New Orleans was fought on January 8, 1815. The night before Jackson was everywhere, encouraging his men.
Wait till you get them in range, boys! Take them as they come!

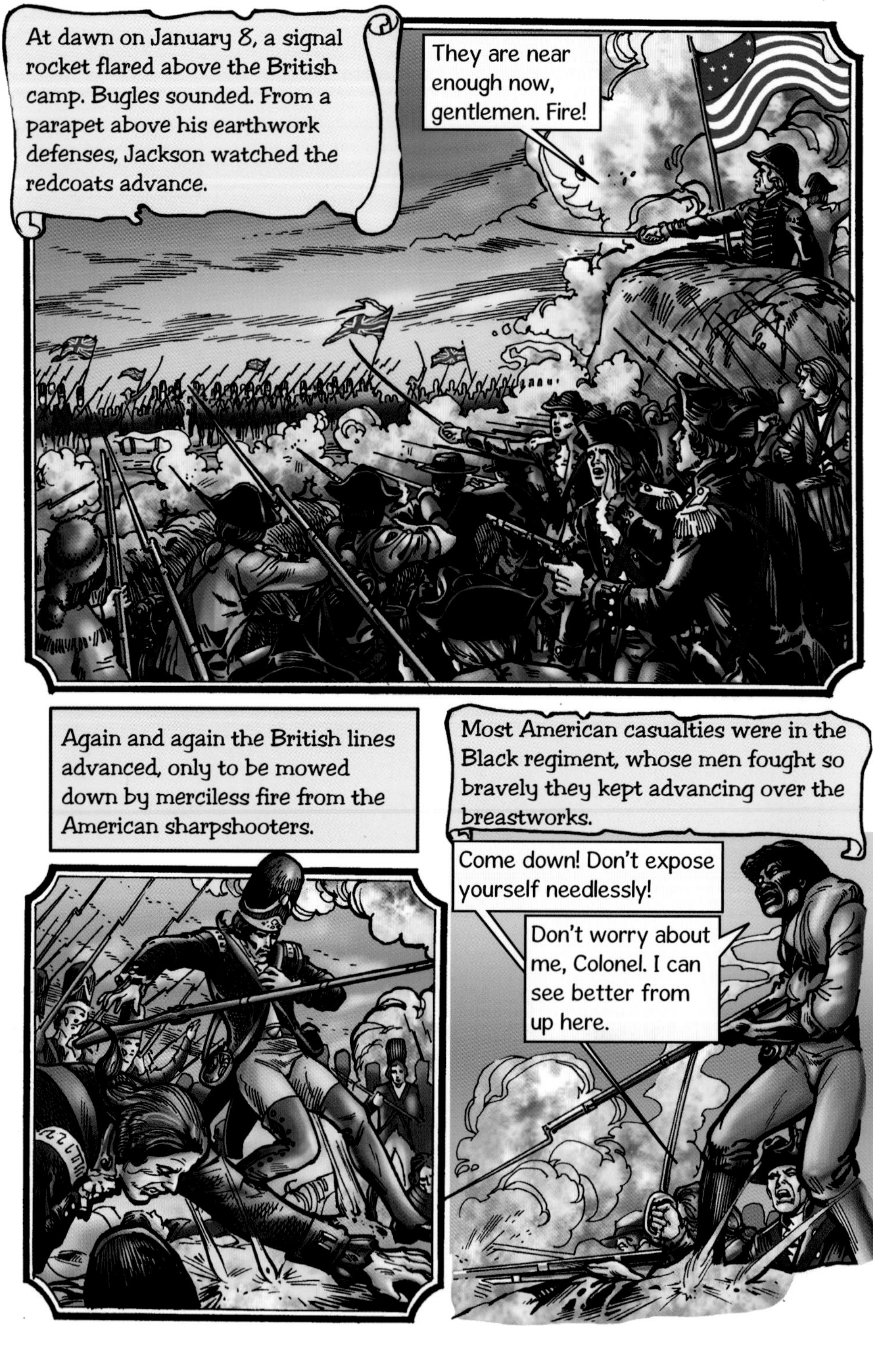
At dawn on January 8, a signal rocket flared above the British camp. Bugles sounded. From a parapet above his earthwork defenses, Jackson watched the redcoats advance.
They are near enough now, gentlemen. Fire!
Again and again the British lines advanced, only to be mowed down by merciless fire from the American sharpshooters.
Most American casualties were in the Black regiment, whose men fought so bravely they kept advancing over the breastworks.
Come down! Don't expose yourself needlessly!
Don't worry about me, Colonel. I can see better from up here.

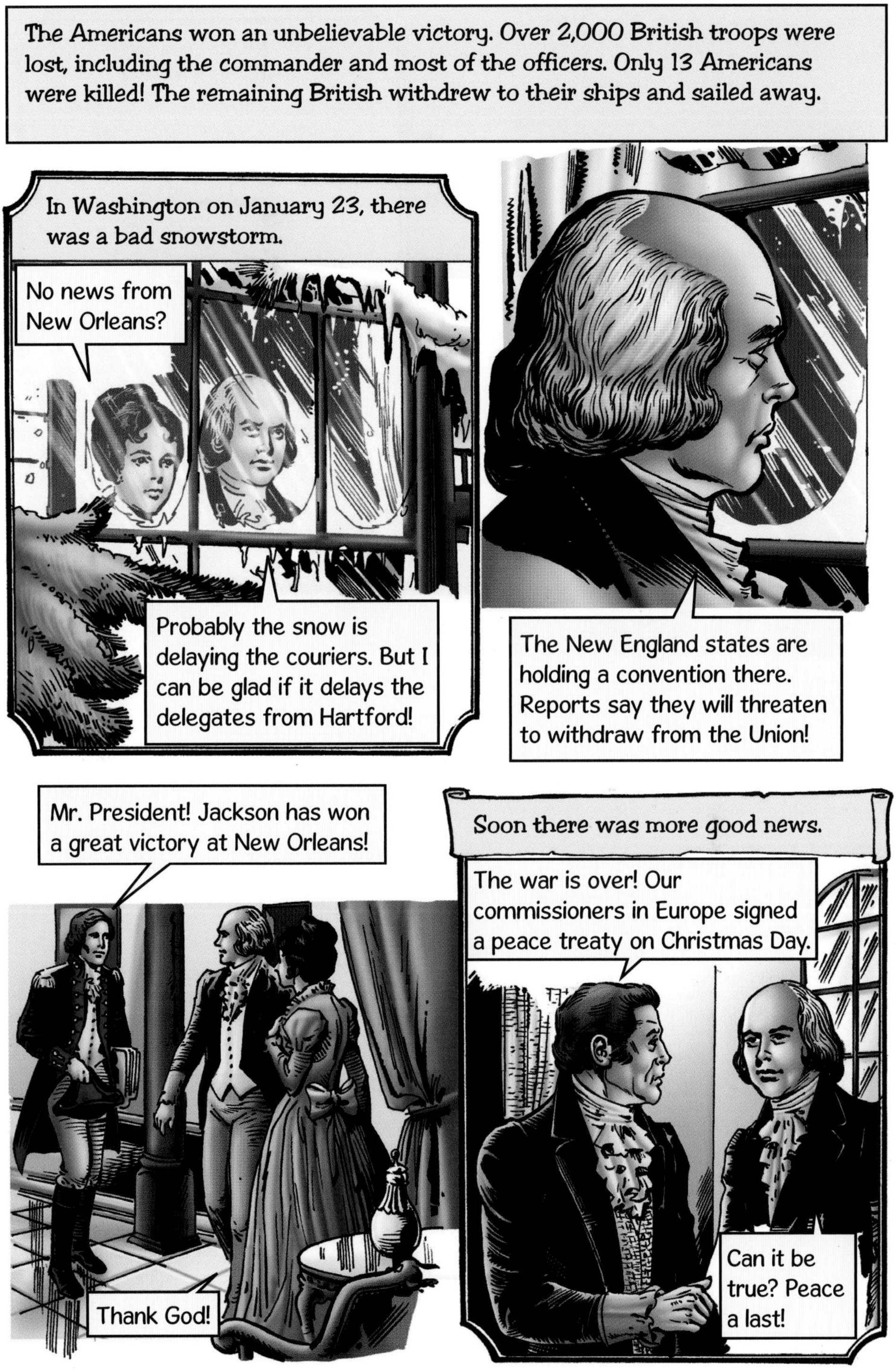
The Americans won an unbelievable victory. Over 2,000 British troops were lost, including the commander and most of the officers. Only 13 Americans were killed! The remaining British withdrew to their ships and sailed away.
In Washington on January 23, there was a bad snowstorm.
No news from New Orleans?
Probably the snow is delaying the couriers. But I can be glad if it delays the delegates from Hartford!
The New England states are holding a convention there. Reports say they will threaten to withdraw from the Union!
Mr. President! Jackson has won a great victory at New Orleans!
Thank God!
Soon there was more good news.
The war is over! Our commissioners in Europe signed a peace treaty on Christmas Day.
Can it be true? Peace a last!

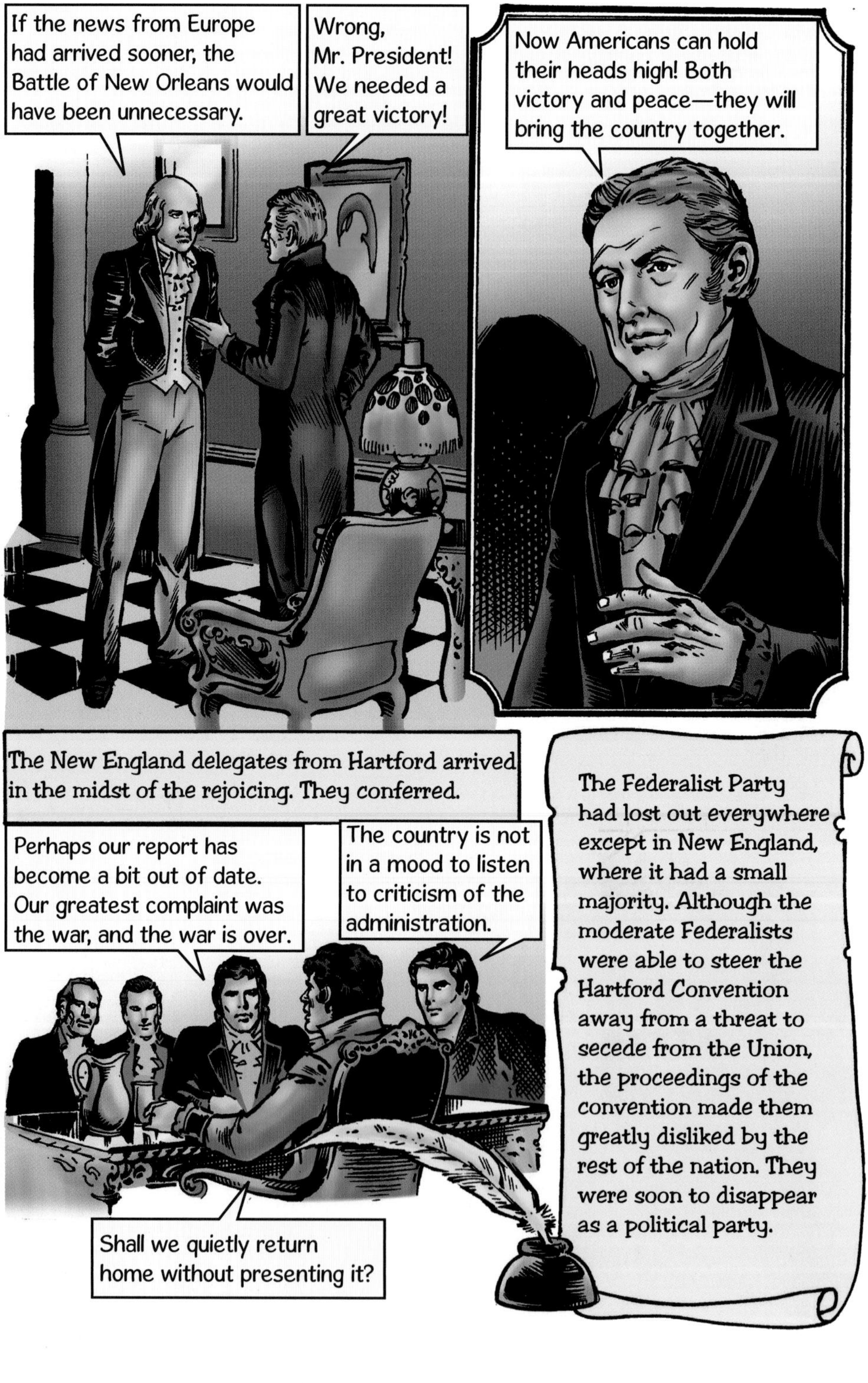
If the news from Europe had arrived sooner, the Battle of New Orleans would have been unnecessary.
Wrong, Mr. President! We needed a great victory!
Now Americans can hold their heads high! Both victory and peace—they will bring the country together.
The New England delegates from Hartford arrived in the midst of the rejoicing. They conferred.
Perhaps our report has become a bit out of date. Our greatest complaint was the war, and the war is over.
The country is not in a mood to listen to criticism of the administration.
Shall we quietly return home without presenting it?
The Federalist Party had lost out everywhere except in New England, where it had a small majority. Although the moderate Federalists were able to steer the Hartford Convention away from a threat to secede from the Union, the proceedings of the convention made them greatly disliked by the rest of the nation. They were soon to disappear as a political party.

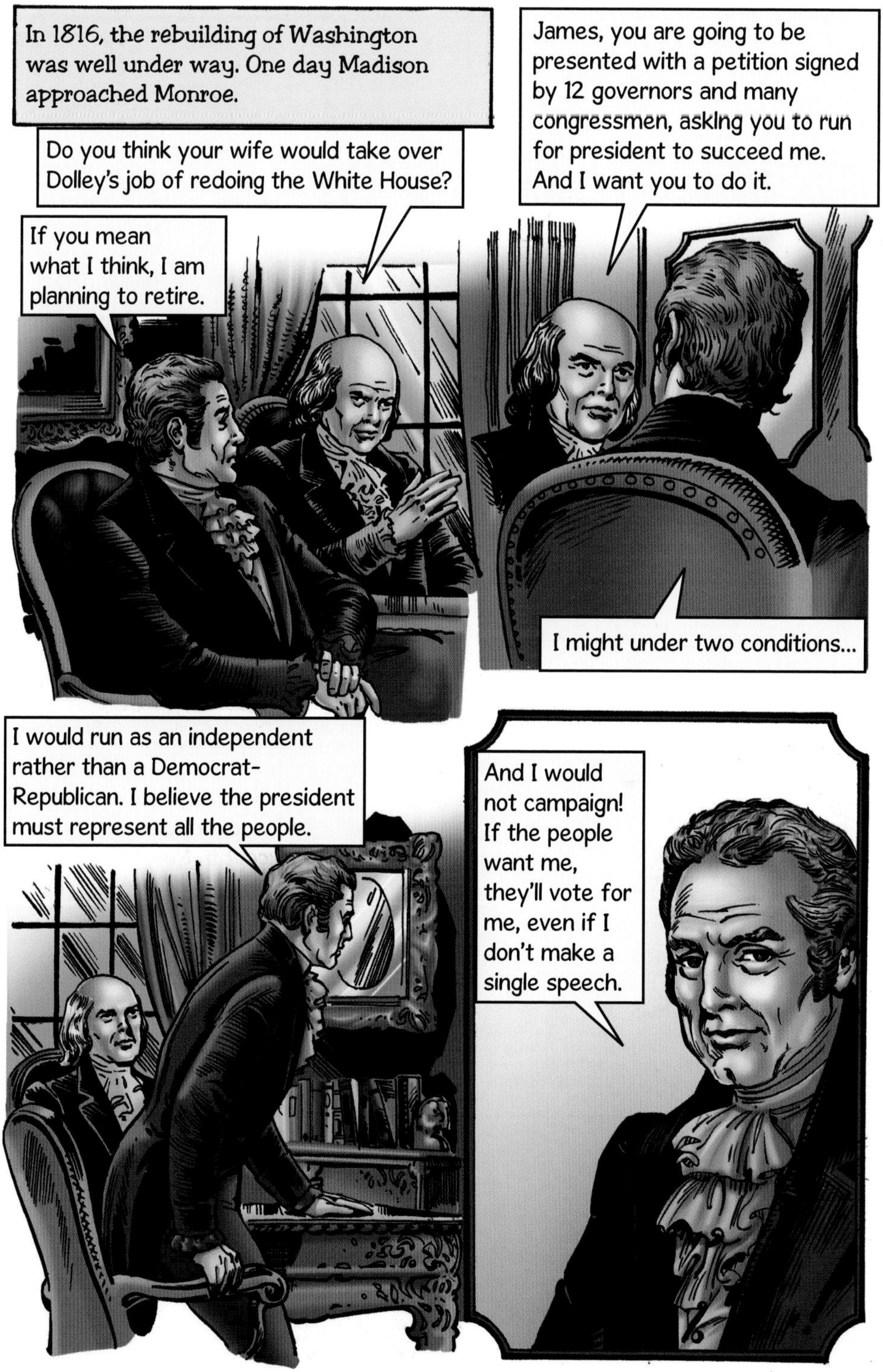
In 1816, the rebuilding of Washington was well under way. One day Madison approached Monroe.
Do you think your wife would take over Dolley's job of redoing the White House?
If you mean what I think, I am planning to retire.
James, you are going to be presented with a petition signed by 12 governors and many congressmen, asking you to run for president to succeed me. And I want you to do it.
I might under two conditions...
I would run as an independent rather than a Democrat-Republican. I believe the president must represent all the people.
And I would not campaign! If the people want me, they'll vote for me, even if I don't make a single speech.

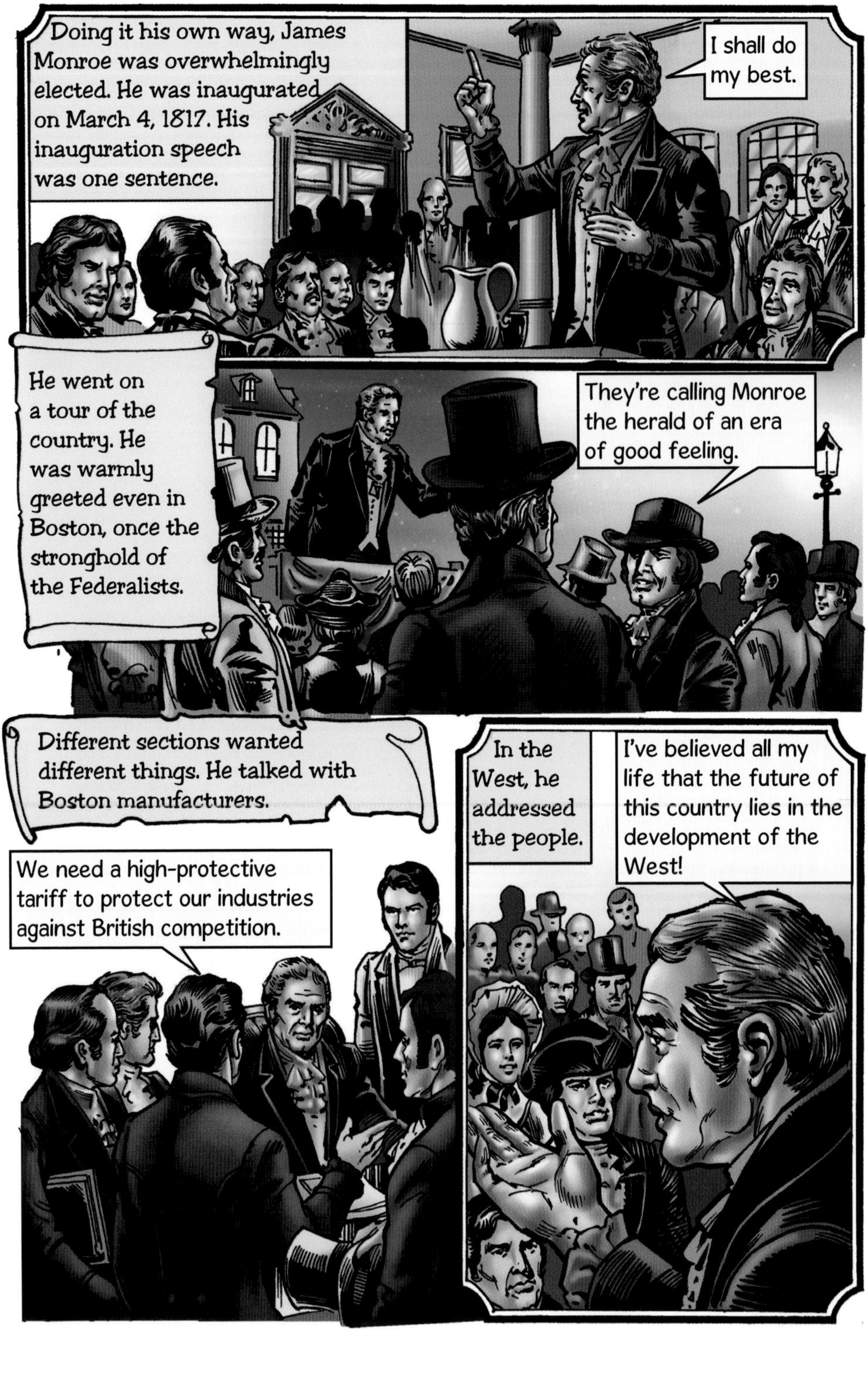
Doing it his own way, James Monroe was overwhelmingly elected. He was inaugurated on March 4, 1817. His inauguration speech was one sentence.
I shall do my best.
He went on a tour of the country. He was warmly greeted even in Boston, once the stronghold of the Federalists.
They're calling Monroe the herald of an era of good feeling.
Different sections wanted different things. He talked with Boston manufacturers.
We need a high-protective tariff to protect our industries against British competition.
In the West, he addressed the people.
I've believed all my life that the future of this country lies in the development of the West!

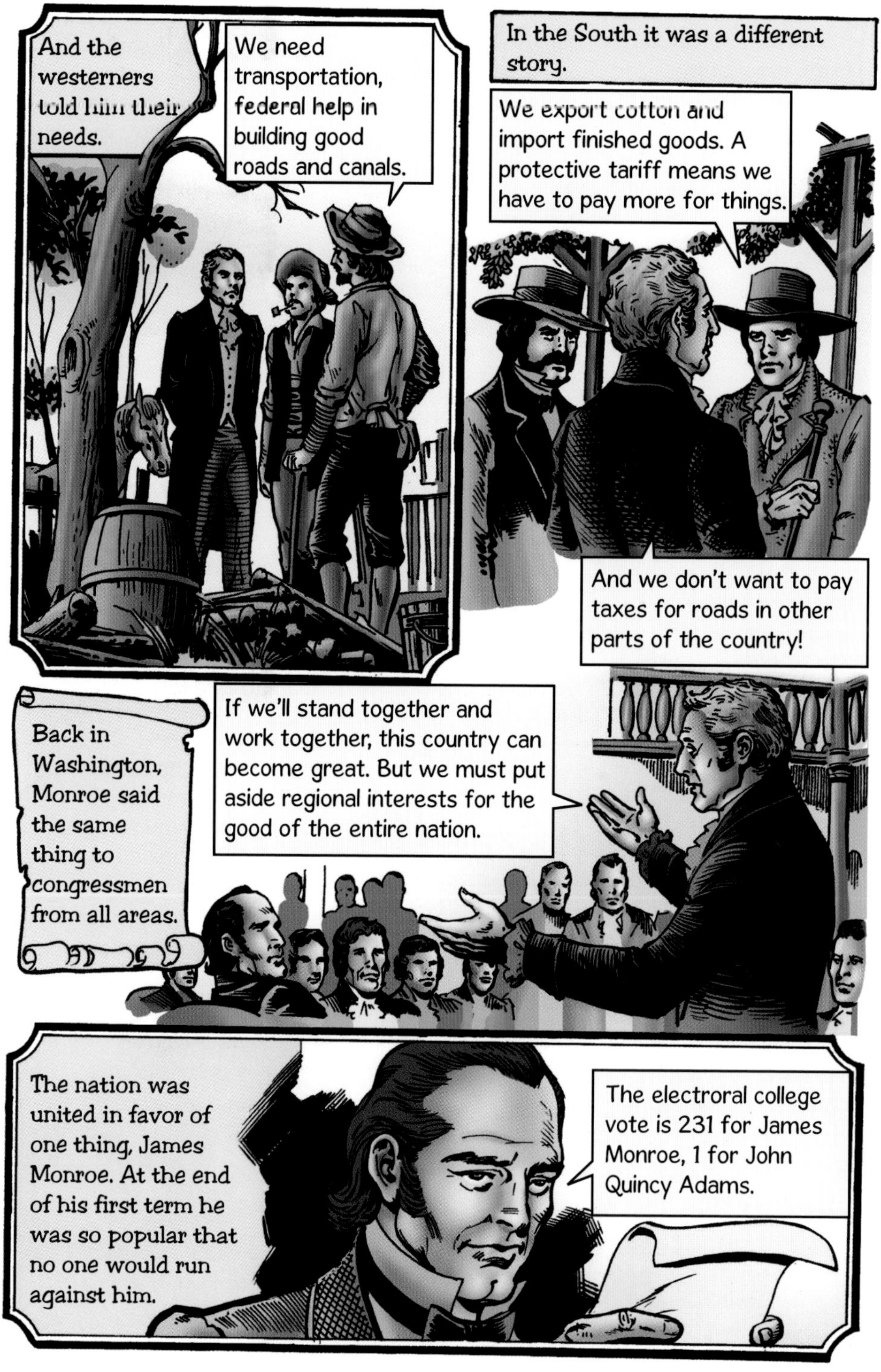
And the westerners told him their needs.
We need transportation, federal help in building good roads and canals.
In the South it was a different story.
We export cotton and import finished goods. A protective tariff means we have to pay more for things.
And we don't want to pay taxes for roads in other parts of the country!
Back in Washington, Monroe said the same thing to congressmen from all areas.
If we'll stand together and work together, this country can become great. But we must put aside regional interests for the good of the entire nation.
The nation was united in favor of one thing, James Monroe. At the end of his first term he was so popular that no one would run against him.
The electroral college vote is 231 for James Monroe, 1 for John Quincy Adams.

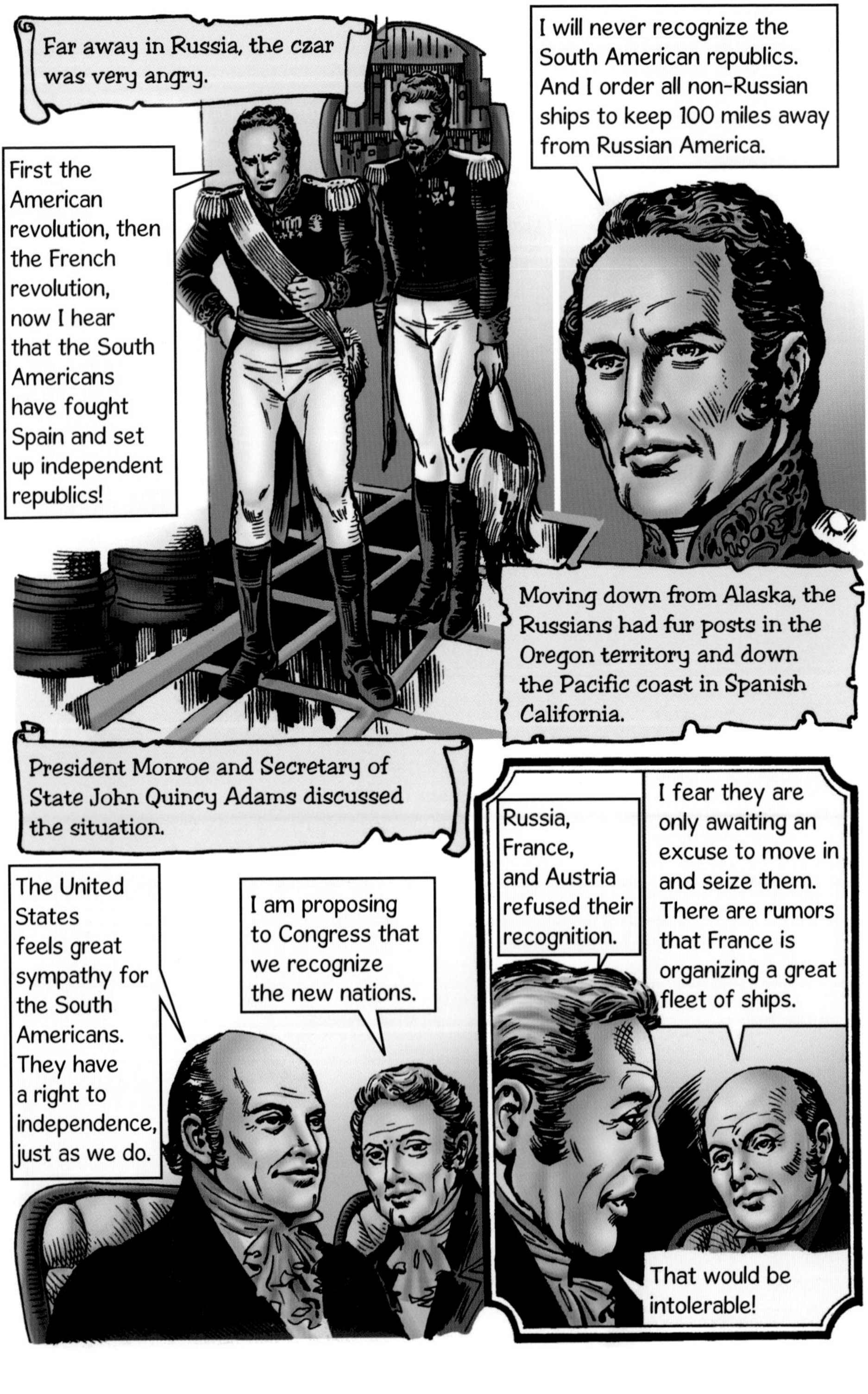

Far away in Russia, the czar was very angry.
First the American revolution, then the French revolution, now I hear that the South Americans have fought Spain and set up independent republics!
I will never recognize the South American republics. And I order all non-Russian ships to keep 100 miles away from Russian America.
Moving down from Alaska, the Russians had fur posts in the Oregon territory and down the Pacific coast in Spanish California.
President Monroe and Secretary of State John Quincy Adams discussed the situation.
The United States feels great sympathy for the South Americans. They have a right to independence, just as we do.
I am proposing to Congress that we recognize the new nations.
Russia, France, and Austria refused their recognition.
I fear they are only awaiting an excuse to move in and seize them. There are rumors that France is organizing a great fleet of ships.
That would be intolerable!

A weak Spain on our borders has caused us enough trouble. A strong France would threaten our security!

What do you suggest we do Mr. President?

The outcome of their deliberations was a policy statement in President Monroe's annual message to Congress.

The American continents are henceforth not to be considered as subjects for future colonization by any European powers.

We had not and would not interfere with internal affairs in Europe or with existing European colonies, President Monroe explained. But we would consider actions by any European power against "governments who have declared their independence, and maintained it," as "dangerous to our peace and safety." This "keep out" notice became known as the Monroe Doctrine, and has been a keystone of our foreign policy.

John Quincy Adams succeeded Monroe as president.

I, John Quincy Adams ...

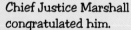

Chief Justice Marshall congratulated him.

Mr. President, I was appointed to my position by your father when he was president of the United States!

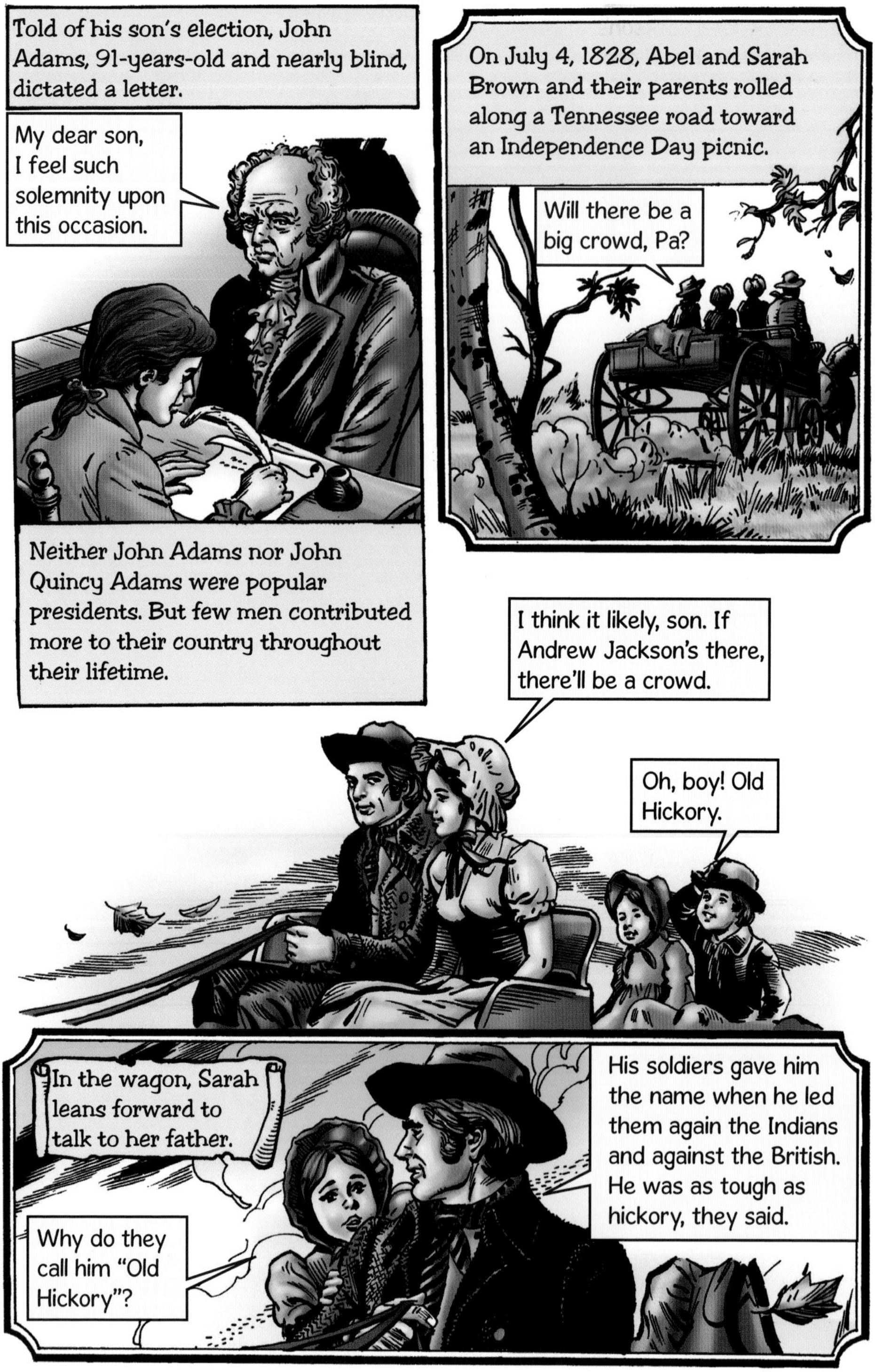
Told of his son's election, John Adams, 91-years-old and nearly blind, dictated a letter.
My dear son, I feel such solemnity upon this occasion.
Neither John Adams nor John Quincy Adams were popular presidents. But few men contributed more to their country throughout their lifetime.
On July 4, 1828, Abel and Sarah Brown and their parents rolled along a Tennessee road toward an Independence Day picnic.
Will there be a big crowd, Pa?
I think it likely, son. If Andrew Jackson's there, there'll be a crowd.
Oh, boy! Old Hickory.
In the wagon, Sarah leans forward to talk to her father.
Why do they call him "Old Hickory"?
His soldiers gave him the name when he led them again the Indians and against the British. He was as tough as hickory, they said.

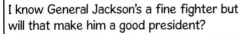

I know General Jackson's a fine fighter but will that make him a good president?

No doubt the speakers today will give plenty of reasons to vote for him.

My reason is simple, he's a man who'll fight for the people of the country—the working man!

Arriving at the picnic, the Browns found a crowd of thousands, and the delicious smell of meat being roasted on spits.

Mrs. Brown joined the women.

Let me help. I brought my plates.

Sarah helped shuck the mounds of corn that would be roasted.

This should be enough to feed an army.

A hungry army.

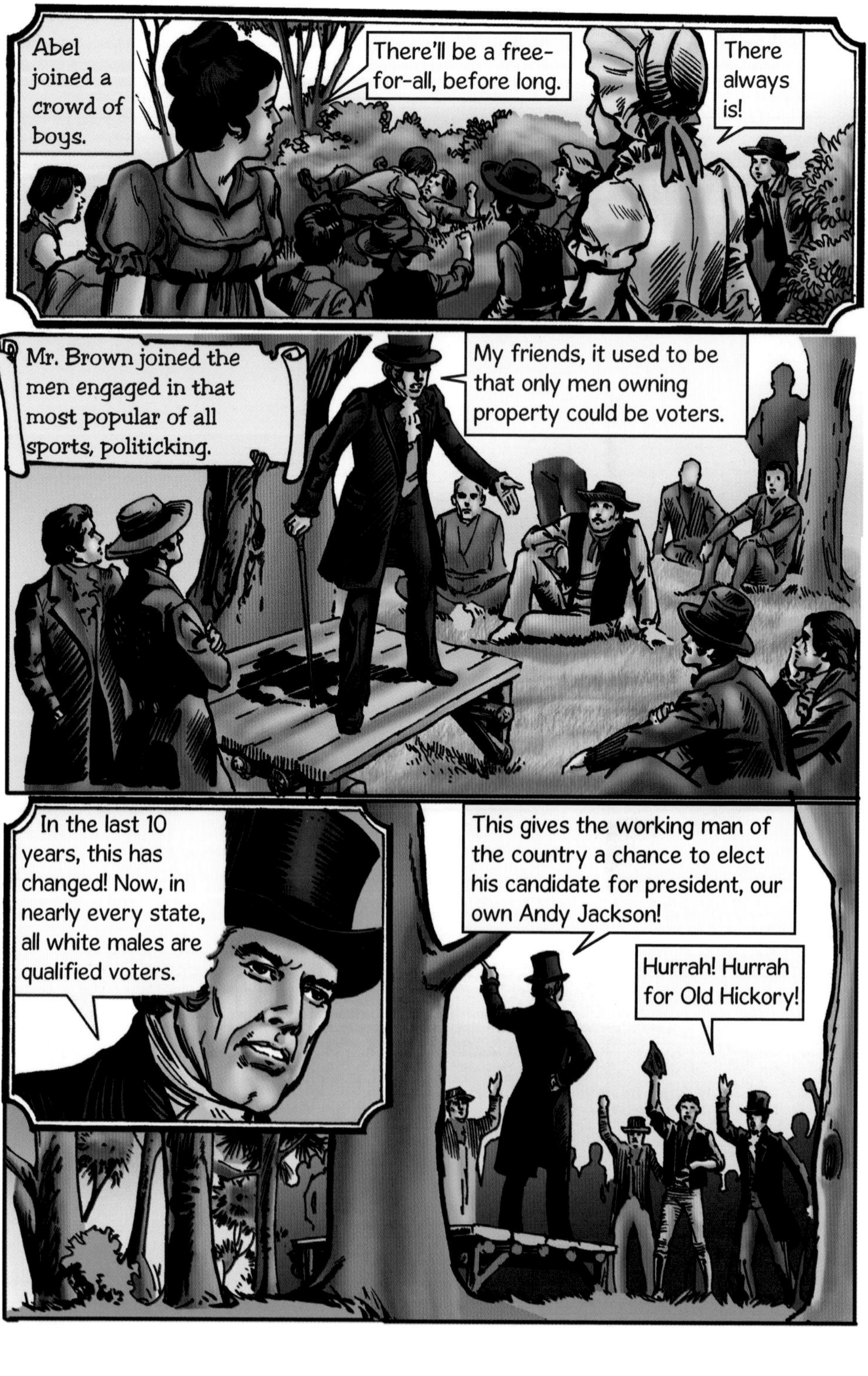
Abel joined a crowd of boys.
There'll be a free-for-all, before long.
There always is!
Mr. Brown joined the men engaged in that most popular of all sports, politicking.
My friends, it used to be that only men owning property could be voters.
In the last 10 years, this has changed! Now, in nearly every state, all white males are qualified voters.
This gives the working man of the country a chance to elect his candidate for president, our own Andy Jackson!
Hurrah! Hurrah for Old Hickory!

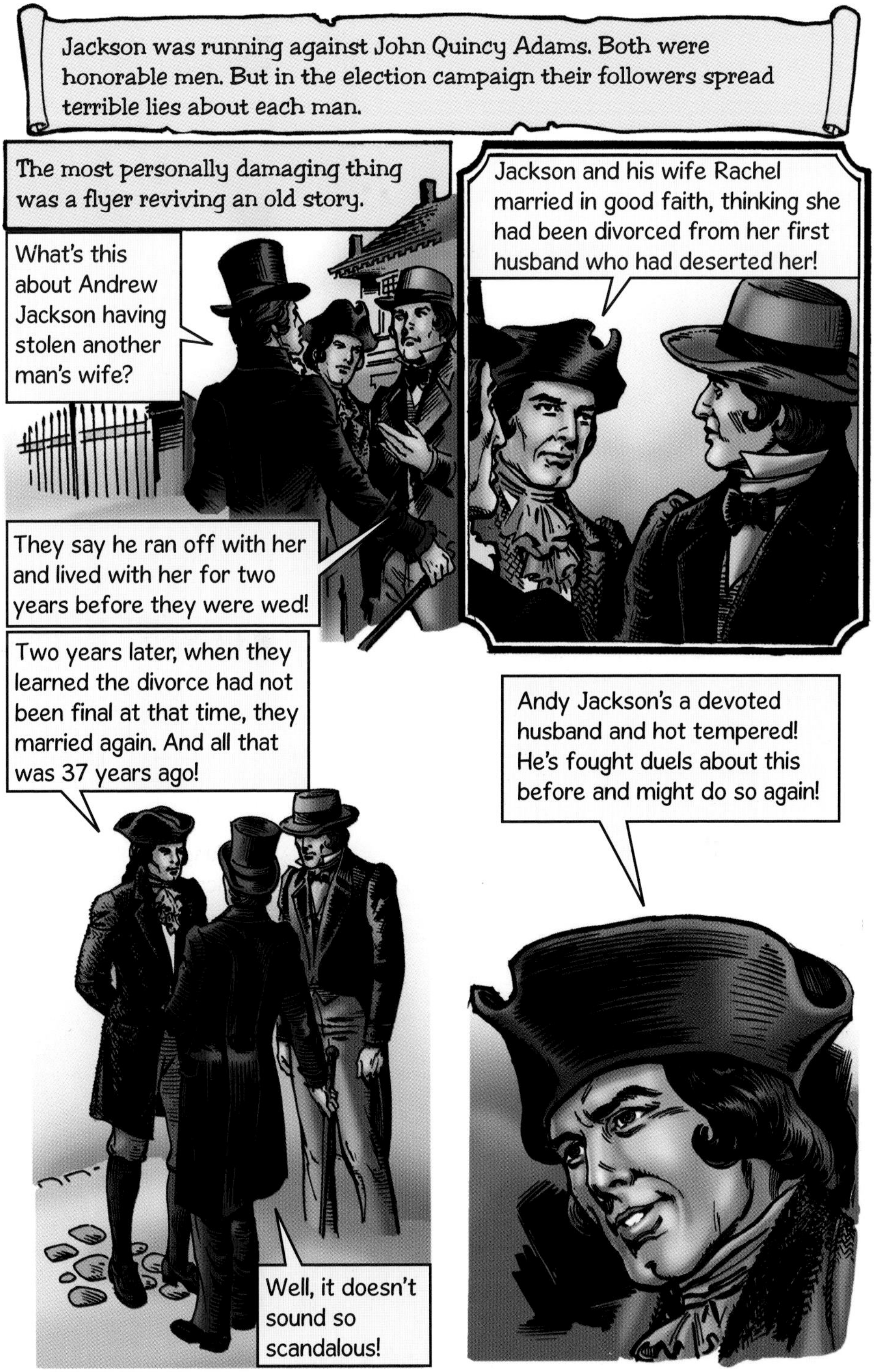
Jackson was running against John Quincy Adams. Both were honorable men. But in the election campaign their followers spread terrible lies about each man.
The most personally damaging thing was a flyer reviving an old story.
What's this about Andrew Jackson having stolen another man's wife?
They say he ran off with her and lived with her for two years before they were wed!
Jackson and his wife Rachel married in good faith, thinking she had been divorced from her first husband who had deserted her!
Two years later, when they learned the divorce had not been final at that time, they married again. And all that was 37 years ago!
Well, it doesn't sound so scandalous!
Andy Jackson's a devoted husband and hot tempered! He's fought duels about this before and might do so again!

When Jackson saw the flyer, his son Jack Donelson, tried to calm him down.

I've never tolerated a smear on your mother's good name, and I won't start now!

Father, dozens of men are involved in printing this—maybe hundreds.

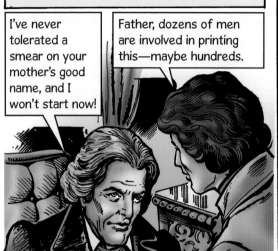

Do you mean to fight all of them?

If need be, yes!

Only Rachel herself was finally able to persuade Jackson not to fight.

You carry enough bullets in your body because of me! And the more you make of this the more people will gossip.

We've been married 37 years and people have whispered nasty things for 36 of them. There's been enough fuss made!

I'll abide by your wishes, ma'am.

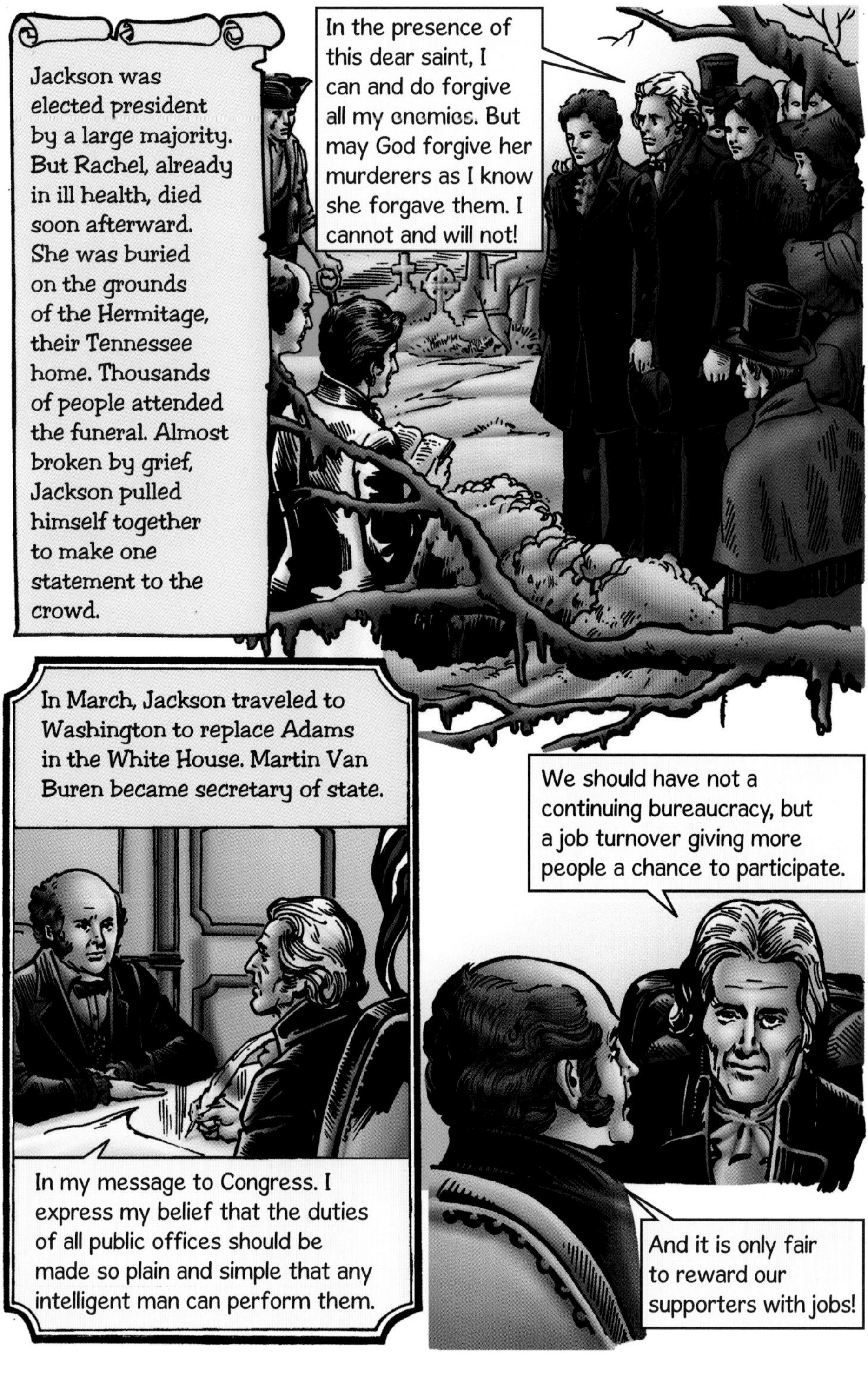
Jackson was elected president by a large majority. But Rachel, already in ill health, died soon afterward. She was buried on the grounds of the Hermitage, their Tennessee home. Thousands of people attended the funeral. Almost broken by grief, Jackson pulled himself together to make one statement to the crowd.
In the presence of this dear saint, I can and do forgive all my enemies. But may God forgive her murderers as I know she forgave them. I cannot and will not!
In March, Jackson traveled to Washington to replace Adams in the White House. Martin Van Buren became secretary of state.
In my message to Congress. I express my belief that the duties of all public offices should be made so plain and simple that any intelligent man can perform them.
We should have not a continuing bureaucracy, but a job turnover giving more people a chance to participate.
And it is only fair to reward our supporters with jobs!

Some Washington office-holders saw it differently.

I'm being fired to make way for one of Jackson's western friends!

I came out for Jackson before the election. That should save me!

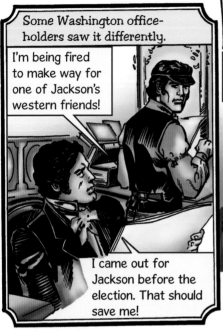

In South Carolina, people hated the protective tariff voted by Congress.

Most everything we buy comes from England—and costs more because of that abominable tariff!

I go along with Calhoun's doctrine of nullification.

John C. Calhoun of South Carolina was the vice president and an advocate of states' rights.

If a state convention decides that an act of Congress is unconstitutional, the state can prevent enforcement of that act within the state!

Then a state can nullify the acts of the national government!

The people in favor of nullification arranged a formal dinner party.

If we arrange a long series of toasts favoring states' rights, perhaps the president will be carried along to make one of his own.

As a Southerner, he should be in favor.

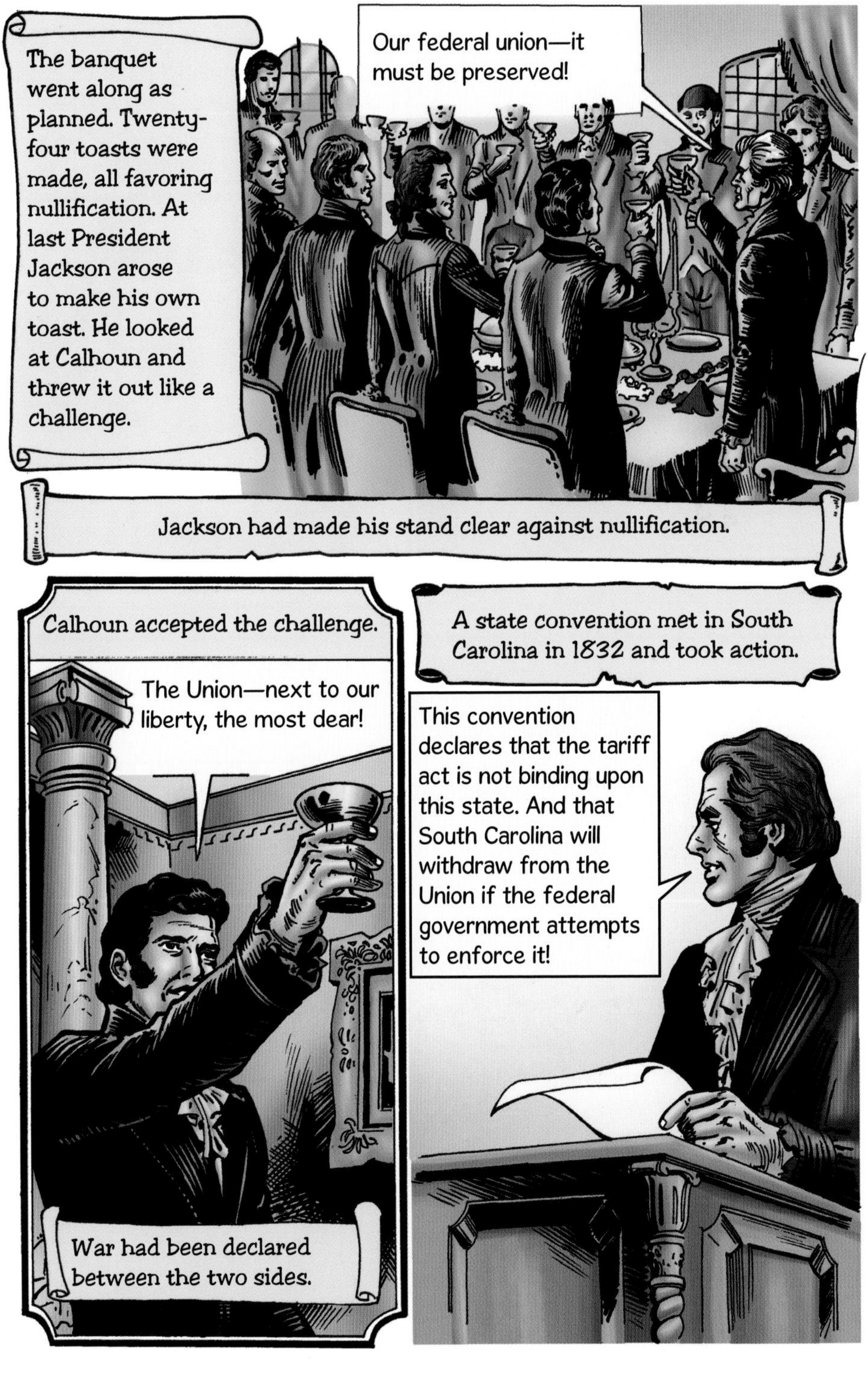
The banquet went along as planned. Twenty-four toasts were made, all favoring nullification. At last President Jackson arose to make his own toast. He looked at Calhoun and threw it out like a challenge.
Our federal union—it must be preserved!
Jackson had made his stand clear against nullification.
Calhoun accepted the challenge.
The Union—next to our liberty, the most dear!
War had been declared between the two sides.
A state convention met in South Carolina in 1832 and took action.
This convention declares that the tariff act is not binding upon this state. And that South Carolina will withdraw from the Union if the federal government attempts to enforce it!

President Jackson did not hesitate to act.

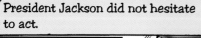

I am reinforcing Forts Moultrie and Sumter, and ordering revenue cutters to stand by ... but we need a compromise solution.

South Carolina, lacking support from other states, repealed its nullification decision. For the time being, the matter was settled peacefully. But Jackson made a prophecy.

Henry Clay worked out a compromise tariff act reducing the rates and rushed it through Congress.

The next pretext for secession will be the slavery question.

At the end of Jackson's second term of office, a group of his cabinet members gathered with him for an informal evening.

What do you think was your greatest accomplishment, Mr. President?

The destruction of the Bank of the United States—that monster that threatened to destroy our republican institutions! The people backed me up, too, and defeated Henry Clay when he ran against me in favor of the Bank!

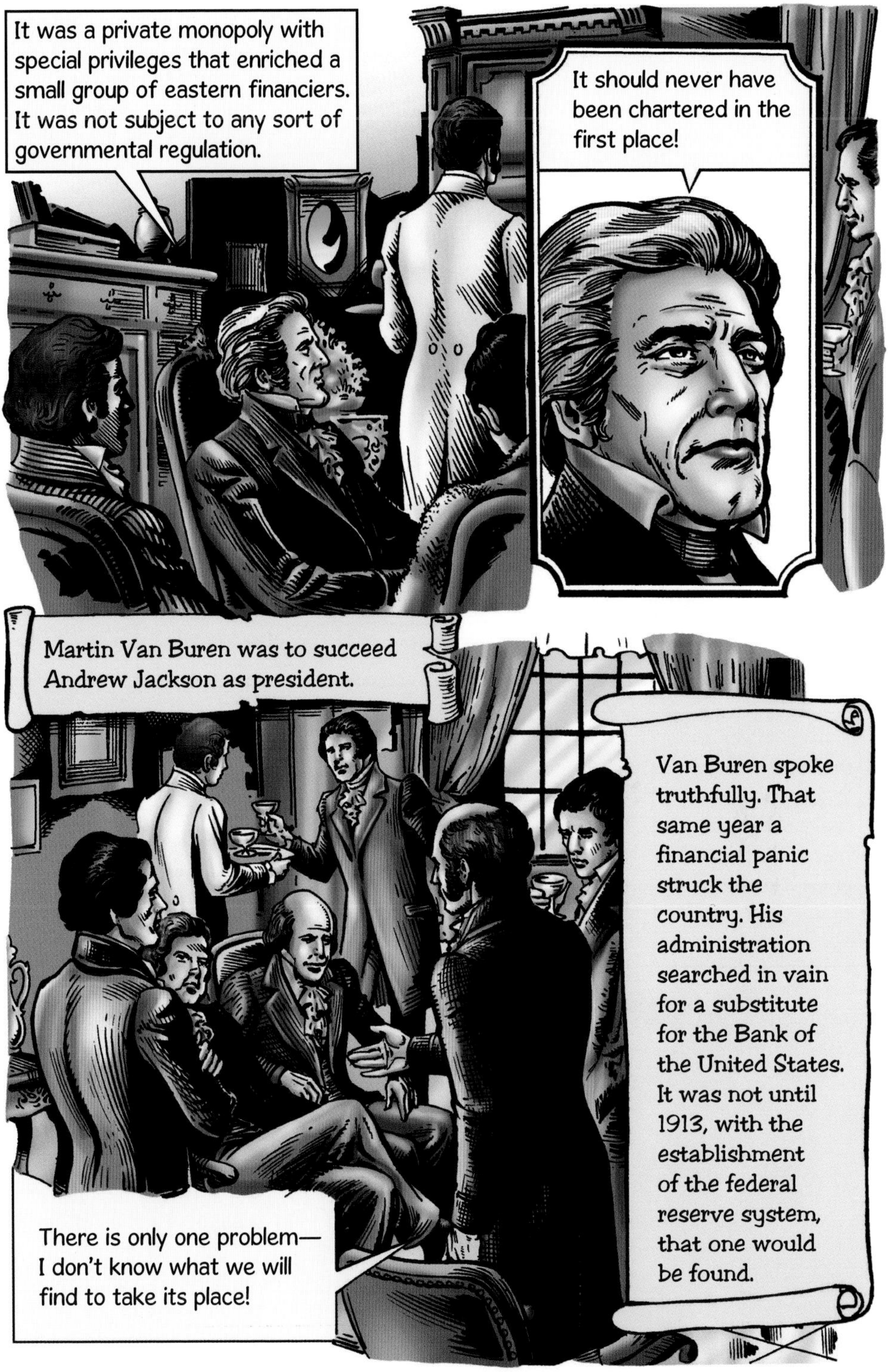
It was a private monopoly with special privileges that enriched a small group of eastern financiers. It was not subject to any sort of governmental regulation.
It should never have been chartered in the first place!
Martin Van Buren was to succeed Andrew Jackson as president.
There is only one problem—I don't know what we will find to take its place!
Van Buren spoke truthfully. That same year a financial panic struck the country. His administration searched in vain for a substitute for the Bank of the United States. It was not until 1913, with the establishment of the federal reserve system, that one would be found.

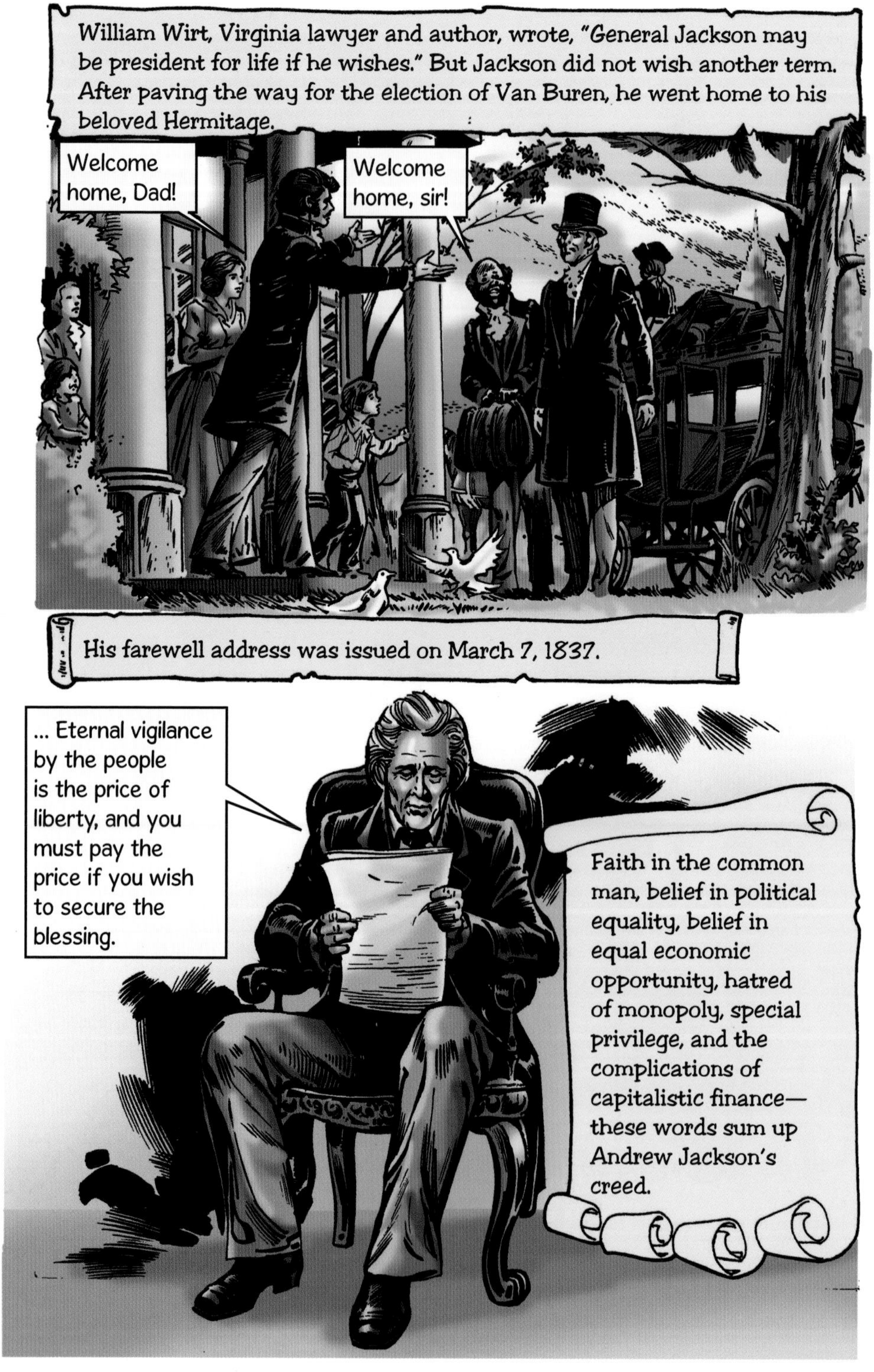
William Wirt, Virginia lawyer and author, wrote, "General Jackson may be president for life if he wishes." But Jackson did not wish another term. After paving the way for the election of Van Buren, he went home to his beloved Hermitage.
Welcome home, Dad!
Welcome home, sir!
His farewell address was issued on March 7, 1837.
... Eternal vigilance by the people is the price of liberty, and you must pay the price if you wish to secure the blessing.
Faith in the common man, belief in political equality, belief in equal economic opportunity, hatred of monopoly, special privilege, and the complications of capitalistic finance—these words sum up Andrew Jackson's creed.